LEAVING A CAREER TO FOLLOW A CALL

A VOCATIONAL GUIDE TO THE ORDAINED MINISTRY

Michael A. Milton, Ph.D.

With an Introduction by Dr. D. James Kennedy

Wipf and Stock Publishers
150 West Broadway • Eugene OR 97401

Wipf and Stock Publishers
150 West Broadway
Eugene, Oregon 97401

Leaving a Career to Follow a Call
A Vocational Guide to the Ministry
By Milton, Michael A.
©2000 Milton, Michael A.
ISBN: 1-57910-347-2
Publication date: July, 2000
Previously published by NPP, 2000.

The text for this book was set in the Weiss font.

But this I do believe (and I will gladly listen to any objection, although I will not believe it) that at each man's birth there comes into being an eternal vocation for him, expressly for him. To be true to himself in relation to this eternal vocation is the highest thing a man can practice...

—Sören Kierkegaard, Purity of Heart is to Will One Thing

To the Glory of the God who still calls,
With love to Mae and John Michael—and all our children,
And in Memory of the one who introduced me to the Lord:
Aunt Eva

CONTENTS

PREFACE vii

ACKNOWLEDGMENTS ix

INTRODUCTION x

1 VOCATION 12

2 REFLECTION 16

3 MODELS 20

4 ISSUES 28

5 RESPONSE 32

6 TRANSITION 41

7 IDENTITY 56

Why Young Men Don't Go Into The Ministry 58

The Ministry Of A Seminarian 64

What Color Is Your Pulpit? 70

Post Seminary Stress Syndrome 81

LEAVING A CAREER TO FOLLOW A CALL

How To Lose Your Ministry While Excelling In Your Profession 90

The Justification Of Preaching 101

God Is Calling Faithful Men 130

Some Further Reading Prior To Seminary 131

INDEX 134

BIBLIOGRAPHY 141

ABOUT THE AUTHOR 147

PREFACE

I think I understand the need for this book.

I personally left a "career" to follow a "call" to the ordained ministry, myself. In my own journey from being a middle manager in a Fortune 500 chemical company to seminarian to pastoral intern to church planter, pastor, and later to becoming the administrator of a seminary which works closely with ministerial candidates, I have learned a few things that can, I pray, be shared with others—for their benefit, and for the benefit of the Church. My goals in writing this book were three-fold:

First, I seek to add a contemporary reflection on the whole issue of vocation from a Biblical and practical perspective. I don't pretend to compare my brief chapter on the issue to (what I consider to be) the standard book on the matter, Edmund Clowney's excellent Called to the Ministry. Rather, I want to digest his conclusions and apply them to our particular situation in these infant years of the twenty-first century. From my conversations and counseling opportunities with others, I am convinced that there is a persistent confusion about the whole issue. Somewhere between egalitarianism and clericalism, there is Biblical truth about vocation that needs to be sounded loudly today.

Second, it is my hope that this book would encourage that certain man and his wife (and children) who are coming face to face with the possible reality that God might be calling him to the ordained ministry. How well my wife and I recall those late nights where we lay in bed talking about what might happen if I surrendered to a call to the ministry. There was a simultaneous feeling of exhilaration over surrendering to what one feels is the "right thing to do" and a cold reality (usually advanced by well-meaning relatives) that doing the "right thing" could mean throwing away a great career (thus financial security) and even an important ministry as an active layman. Moods alternate between fear and fanaticism during those times. It is a time of prayer and, in retrospect, will become a sacred season of growth. Couples going through that time, though, need some real pastoral encouragement. This book most certainly aims to provide that.

Third, Leaving a Career to Follow a Call is intended to be a practical guide for those committed to following a track that culminates in the ordained ministry of their Church (whatever your denomination or affiliation might be). It is my experience that whether one is leaving a career as a banker to become a Baptist minister or leaving a career as a construction worker to become an Episcopal priest, there are considerable similarities. Indeed, the whole matter of candidacy, for the most part, is simply variations on a theme. The truth is, though, that much of the denominational candidacy policies in place are there for the old "traditional" candidate—the single student who was called at age sixteen and who passed from high school to university to seeking a seminary. The model of a typical seminarian has changed dramatically and that candidate of many denominational guidebooks is no longer the norm, though he is an important model (I have added a chapter called "Why Young Men Don't Go into the Ministry" to address this trend). The new traditional student looks like you probably do: in his thirties or forties with a family to feed and with one (and sometimes two) careers already under his belt.

I have made this book as a guide for you.

—Michael A. Milton
April 5, 2000

ACKNOWLEDGMENTS

This book goes to publication and, prayerfully and hopefully, into the hands of those who need it, with deep appreciation for the many people who have assisted me.

I want to thank Mrs. Ellen Smith and Mrs. Laura Lee Sims for their editorial assistance. While they did stellar work, any remaining errors in this book are mine.

I am and ever shall be greatly indebted to The Rev. Robert E. Baxter and The Rev. Dr. D. James Kennedy for modeling and teaching me what being a Minister of the Gospel is really all about and, thus, providing me the model for writing a book like this.

I thank my secretary, Mrs. Agnes Cooper, for her tireless work in seeking to maximize my ministry.

I am particularly appreciative of my session and our congregation at Kirk O' the Isles Presbyterian Church, Savannah, Georgia, for their Kingdom vision. It is a joy to try and practice what I preach in this book in their gracious presence. I also have been honored to have served the saints at Redeemer Presbyterian Church in Overland Park, Kansas as well as students at Knox Seminary and Erskine Seminary. I am grateful for God having used His saints at each of those wonderful places to sanctify and bless me for the work of the ministry.

Dr. David Calhoun of Covenant Theological Seminary provided me with a copy of The Southern Presbyterian Review, Number II, September, 1848, which provided further scholarly insight into the matter of The Call to Ministry. Thanks to him and to Dr. L. Roy Taylor for their words of support.

Finally, I wish to thank my wife, Mae, for her faithfulness to me throughout this gift of life and for her constant support on this project in particular. Thank you, John Michael, my dear little boy, for always greeting me with a hug every day. What a source of joy you are!

INTRODUCTION

BY

DR. D. JAMES KENNEDY
Senior Minister
Coral Ridge Presbyterian Church, Fort Lauderdale, Florida

It would be impossible for me to consider writing the introduction to this book about leaving one's successful career to follow a call into the ministry without recalling vividly how that very experience changed the entire course of my life. Granted, I was not the CEO of a Fortune 500 corporation in my 40's or 50's when the call came; as a matter of fact, I was a young fellow in my early 20's who had been a Christian only a few short years.

But, regardless of my age, there was that "mystic, supernatural touch of God which comes with His call," as Oswald Chambers characterizes it. and I was successful—tremendously so in my own eyes. With none other than the famous Arthur Murray as my hero, my mentor, and my employer, I had risen to the position of manager of his Tampa dance studio. I had even taken first place in his All-American Arthur Murray Dance Instructor Competition, and was chosen to serve on his National Dance Board to assist in the creation of new steps for the instructional program.

and it was paying very, very well. I could see no reason why I should not become, like Arthur Murray himself, a millionaire, especially in view of the fact that I was asked to take over the studio in Sarasota, Florida, not only as manager but as half-owner! My career seemed to be set in concrete. But then came that bombshell which is the well-handled subject of this book by Michael Milton: the call to preach the Gospel, regardless of what career opportunities might seem to beckon ahead.

The struggle that ensued was of Herculean proportions. It was physical as well as spiritual, I remember so clearly, as I neared the point of utter desperation, kneeling at my desk in the dance studio, then slumping to the floor until I was stretched out full-length, asking face down, "What do you want me to do, Lord? Do you really want me to quit this job? Are you sure you want to use somebody like me?" Like Jacob at the ford Jabbock, I was caught in a gigantic wrestling match between self-preservation in a secure career and surrender to the unknown and the unpredictable. Perhaps you know who won both fights.

I go into this much detail about myself only because Mike Milton requested I say something about my own leaving a career to follow a call, and also to underscore the appropriateness and the practical usefulness of a book entitled, Leaving a Career to Follow a Call. Dr. Milton provides many Scriptural, anecdotal, and didactic illustrations of just how real—and sometimes how agonizing—the decision-making process can become when God reaches through the protective screen of a man's "chosen" work and lifestyle when they happen to be on a collision course with His sovereign will.

That call led not only to the pastoral ministry, but also to the establishment of Knox Theological Seminary where Mike Milton was our first graduate. He subsequently was employed by Knox Seminary in an administrative and student-recruitment capacity. It has been most heartwarming to see the way that God is using him.

Leaving my career and following my call was indeed the most wonderful thing I ever did. The mind of man will never comprehend the wonder, the mystery, or the operational ramifications of this miracle we know as "the call." But the pages that follow will assuredly add more to the reader's understanding and appreciation of this sacred encounter with the Holy Spirit than before.

1

VOCATION

A THEOLOGY OF CALLING
FOR THOSE WHO ALREADY HAVE ONE

When we say "Leaving a Career to Follow a Call" what do we mean and what are we implying?

The Latin, vocare, from whence we get our English vocation, means to call, to summon. When we speak of vocation, then, in this book, we are speaking of one's calling in life. There are some wonderful books on calling. Edmund Clowney's Called to the Ministry is perhaps the best of the bunch.[1] I will not go too deeply into that subject, but do want to make several general comments before moving to what I think is a much-needed Theology of Vocation for those already in a career.

THE BIBLICAL UNDERSTANDING OF CALLING

In the Word of God, there is a General Call and an Effectual Call and what we might define as a Technical Call. God gives the General Call to every creature on earth. We are all called to turn from our sins and to turn to God and His Plan for our salvation. This is the "fundamental prerequisite for the performance of any Christian service."[2] We are all called to live according to His Law; we are all called to a life of service to God and our fellow man. So, every Christian—indeed, every person on earth, has a calling of a sort—a General Call (Calvinists like myself believe there is also an effectual calling in which the Holy Spirit improves the General Call and makes it effective unto salvation). Then, we may also observe

---

[1] See the Reading List at the end of this book. For a scholarly treatment of the minister's call, see The Southern Presbyterian Review, No. II, September, 1848, "The Call to the Ministry—Its Nature and Evidence."

[2] Samuel T. Logan, Jr., ed., "The Minister's Call" by Joel Nederhood, The Preacher and Preaching: Reviving the Art in the Twentieth Century (Philipsburg, NJ: Presbyterian and Reformed Publishing Company, 1986), 45.

from the Bible a Technical Call. This is a calling related to one's life's work. John Calvin wrote that

> Finally, this point is to be noted: the Lord bids each one of us in all life's actions to look to his calling. For He knows with what great restlessness human nature flames, with what fickleness it is borne hither and thither, how its ambition longs to embrace various things at once. Therefore, lest through our stupidity and rashness everything be turned topsy-turvy, he has appointed duties for every man in his particular way of life. and that no one may thoughtlessly transgress his limits, he has named those various kinds of livings 'callings.' Therefore each individual has his own kind of living assigned to him by the Lord as a sort of sentry post, so that he may not heedlessly wander about throughout life.[3]

Calvin taught that all men and women have a calling in life and it is their duty to investigate the gifts and circumstances of their lives to discover and exercise that calling to the glory of God. Of course, this doctrine brought enormous joy to the humble workers of that day, as it should today. Yet, within that broader Technical Calling, there are those who are a part of His Kingdom (those who have received an Effectual Call) who are called to a certain peculiar work in the Kingdom. Some are called to go and journey to another land (like Abraham). Others receive a Technical Call to bear the Son of God (only one of those: Mary). Others, and this is our concern, having been called to repentance and faith, having been summoned by God Himself, then, to be a part of His Kingdom, receive a Technical Call to preach and minister in His Name. Among those we would include the Prophets and the Apostles.

A powerful example of one who knew he had this Technical Call was the Old Testament prophet Amos. Amos had been called by God to leave his humble rural life to journey to the Northern Kingdom with a Divine warning. At Bethel, the capital of the Northern Kingdom, Amaziah the Priest got wind of Amos' prophecies. He goes to the King, Jeroboam, and conspires to get rid

---

[3] See Institutes of the Christian Religion, III.10.9, John T. McNeil, editor (Philadelphia: The Westminster Press, 1960), and 724-725.

of Amos. "The land is not able to bear all his words." (Amos 7.10). So Amos answers:

> Then Amos answered, and said to Amaziah: 'I was no prophet, Nor was I a son of a prophet, But I was a sheepbreeder and a tender of sycamore fruit.' Then the Lord took me as I followed the flock, and the Lord said to me, 'Go, prophesy to My people Israel.'
>
> Now therefore, hear the word of the Lord... (Amos 7.14-16, NKJV).

Amos grounded his authority to preach to the resistant hearers solely on his Technical Call.

Once, an aging old Nazarene preacher asked me, "Son, are you called?" I said, "I think so." He asked again. "Son, I said, 'Are you called?'" He grew somewhat agitated. So did I. I answered once more, "Yes, I think I am." He then drew closer to me and looked me right in the eye: "Son, you better know you are called. In the end, your call is all you got. When they spread rumors about you, when they reject you, when they betray you, when they run you out of town, the only thing that will stand you in good stead will be that you know that you know that you know...that you are called. Now go home and pray until you know!"

Those were good words. Amos knew. Amos could withstand the pressure of the Priest and the King because he knew that he knew that he knew...that he was called.

So must you know that you are called.

CLARIFICATION OF THE CALL: INWARD AND OUTWARD

John Calvin is helpful to all of us when we come to this point. How do we know we are called? Not many of us will receive a blinding light on a road to Damascus like St. Paul. Not all of us will be in the field on one day and in the pulpit on the next and know we are called. Most of us will go through a process. Calvin tells us that we must have an "Inward Call" and an "Outward Call" working together. In fact, one without the other will invalidate what we might think is a call.

The Inward call is that stirring of God in our hearts, in our deepest persons. It is the Hound of Heaven of Francis Thompson's classic poem.[4] It is a "secret call of which each minister is conscious before God, and which does not have the church as witness. But there is the good witness of our heart that we receive the proffered office not with ambition or avarice, not with any other selfish desire, but with a sincere fear of God and desire to build up the church. That is indeed necessary for each one of us if we would have our ministry approved by God."[5]

The Outward Call is the ordinary, "outward and solemn call which has to do with the public order of the church."[6] It is interesting to me to note that the Outward Call sometimes appears at first in the most humble of means. Often, we who are in the ministry can recall a single comment by, say, an elderly lady in the Sunday School class who remarked, "Son that was wonderful. Have you ever thought about the ministry?" It may happen in another way, but most of us can point to a comment and a situation similar to that, which was a crystallizing event in clarifying our sense of call. Of course, it has to go further than that.

Most denominations are good at helping candidates with clarification of the Outward Call. It takes a great deal of prayer and earnest soul work, though, to clarify the Inward Call. If you are struggling through that as you read, don't give up! Seek the blessing of the Truth for your own life. You will have heard it said, surely, that "if you can do something else other than preach, then, do it. But, if after you have considered all, you say with Paul in 1 Corinthians 9.16, '...for necessity is laid upon me; yea, woe is unto me, if I preach not the gospel!' then come and join this ministry!"

---

[4] See The Hound of Heaven, Francis Thompson with an Introduction by GK Chesterton (Brandon Publishing, 1996)

[5] Institutes, IV.3.10, page 1062-63.

[6] Ibid.

2

REFLECTION

HOW I LEFT A CAREER TO FOLLOW A CALL

I am a child of the Church. Baptized as an infant at Felicity Methodist Episcopal Church in New Orleans, Louisiana, I was subsequently reared at Amite (Southern) Baptist Church in Denham Springs, Louisiana. Following a marked departure from the Lord and the things of God, I pursued a prodigal path that led me, at length, to the harsh awareness that I was eating husks in the hog pen. I did everything wrong and sinful one can do short of getting locked up or getting mixed up in drugs. You can imagine the sordid tales of broken relationships, regrettable decisions and misery which marks so many lives like mine. For me there came a defining moment in that realization of my sin that led me on a spiritual quest for "home." That journey took me on stints as a lay preacher in the United Methodist Church and then later in the Episcopal Church and a return engagement to the Southern Baptist Church. For all of my religious interests, and by then, well seasoned churchmanship, I was still far from the "Father's House," and it was not until I agreed to go to an Evangelism Explosion ("EE") clinic in 1986 that I came to see truly who I was and who God is.

Robert Farrarr Capon wrote that every minister must point to a time when he "...developed...a passion for the Passion."[7] My passion for the Passion came then in Evangelism Explosion. I recognized my own sinfulness, God's holiness, and the love, mercy and grace available in Jesus Christ. I also, for the first time, understood my responsibility to take the Great Commission seriously and to be obedient to it. Indeed, I like to say that at EE, I received "spiritual open heart surgery." I experienced new life in Jesus Christ for the first time and quickly rushed home to tell my wife, Mae. I will never forget the moment that my wife and I knelt beside the sink in our master bath and committed our lives to Jesus Christ as our Lord and to being His servants. That was the beginning. I was home in my

---

[7] Robert Rarrar Capon, The Foolishness of Preaching: Proclaiming the Gospel against the Wisdom of the World (Grand Rapids: Eerdmans, 1998), 8.

relationship to Jesus Christ—but His work with me was just beginning.

I had been an account manager for two Fortune 500 organizations. Within days of my experience at Evangelism Explosion and our new commitment to Christ, I was greeted by my boss at a hastily called airport meeting in which he announced that I had been promoted to a District Manager in Kansas City. My wife and her daughter, whom I had taken to raise as my own, were off to the Midwest.

The influence of reading several Reformed authors brought me into contact with the Presbyterian Church in America (PCA) and so we immediately sought out and joined a PCA church in Olathe, Kansas. There our family was put in an incubator under the fine preaching ministry of a Godly pastor and in the midst of a loving congregation. We learned what the family could be from our pastor, and what the church could be from our fellow parishioners. During that time I became an adult Sunday School teacher, started Evangelism Explosion at that local church, and served in several other ways, as well. My wife taught in the children's ministry and our daughter was active in the youth group. Soon, the people of that church elected me to the office of ruling elder. I was ordained and upon my ordination began to pour myself, joyfully, into the work of the Presbytery and General Assembly of my denomination. There has never been a greater time of growth for my family.

Sometime during that period, I was disturbed in the inner man, once more, by Thompson's divine Hound. Increasingly, I became aware of a gnawing awareness that God had given me a passion for His Word and for His people, those who were found, and especially, in my case those who were still lost and needed to be reached. In addition to the "Hound of Heaven" barking on the inside of me I began to hear remarks like these:

> "That was a great teaching in our class. You know, Mike, I've been meaning to say this for some time: we think...well...we believe that you should be a minister! Our church needs men like you!"

and,

> "Mike, you and Mae are just meant for the ministry!"

Those comments formed an "outer" barking of the "Hound of Heaven."

For me, the inner and outer stimuli were forming an undeniable sense of call to the ministry of Word and Sacrament in the Church.

My first reaction was, "I am not worthy." Then, having convinced myself of that, I did what any other honest Jonah would do: I bought a ticket for Tarshish. Tarshish for me was to be Law school.

I had, of course, told my wife about my sense of call. I told her all of the reasons why I was called, but also assured her that my innate unworthiness would prevent it from going any further. That simple reality, I suggested to her with an air of decisiveness, would cause me to go no further with it.

She just listened. Honestly, I don't think she ever said a word. I hated it when she did that. I wished she had agreed with me. I always got the feeling that she knew better than I did what the outcome would have to be.

So, with a "call" and with "tickets" to the "Tarshish" Law School in hand, I sought to smother the idea of ordained ministry. Of course, the story needs go no further at that point. The process only went so far as an application form before I realized that I was dreadfully unhappy and in fact on the verge of sin by running from God. It was that real to me.

During this period of wrestling with the call, the youth minister at my church suggested I read a book entitled simply, Called to the Ministry by Edmund Clowney. That book, perhaps more than any other, provided the most help in analyzing my situation against others and within the context of Scripture. I felt stronger than ever that I was bound in some sort of holy chains to the Gospel ministry. But, I began to sense, after reading that book, that I would find freedom only in surrendering to life in those chains. For the first time I understood St. Paul's words when he wrote,

> "Woe to me if I preach not the Gospel of Jesus Christ."(1 Cor. 9.16)

I went to speak with my pastor. I told him my story. I told him about the Inward call and Outer Call I was experiencing. I told him about Law School and my attempt to run from God. I told him how I felt that if I failed to pursue this idea of the ministry to its end, whatever that might be, I would feel like I was sinning. I went into great detail with my own testimony and how I felt that I was not the kind of man God would want as a minister. He listened. Then he spoke.

He had seen God's hand on me and believed that God was calling me to the ministry. It would mean a great sacrifice to leave my career as a manager for a Fortune 500 company. It would require the agreement of my wife for such a transition. My past, he assured me, was similar to that of the Apostles and Prophets who had been called out of lives of disobedience and sin into the service of the Savior. He saw no reason why I could not begin the long and arduous process in our denomination of moving to the ordination as a minister of the Gospel.

The only real issue was my commitment to leave my career to follow that call.

He agreed to pray with me about it and to help me in the process when I told him I was ready.

The grace and peace I found in those few moments in that pastor's study has lasted for almost ten years now. I went home, and in tears and told my wife about my meeting with the pastor. She told me that she had always known I was called to the ministry. She had seen my agonizing struggle to come to grips with it. It was, though, something that I had to do. She would be there and would follow me if I surrendered to the Lord. That was my final sense of call.

There would be no turning back.

3

MODELS

THE BIBLICAL CASE FOR A MID-CAREER CHANGE TO THE ORDAINED MINISTRY

Robert N. Rodenmayer, in the Kellogg Lectures at Episcopal Theological School in February of 1958, delivered a series of addresses on the role and work of the modern pastor. In noting how individuals go into the ministry, he had this to say, which is of particular interest to us:

> There are persons who come into the ministry after years of doing something quite different. A man may have thought seriously of this calling years ago and have given it up for a number of reasons. Then he marries, raises his children, and makes a living. But the old vision persists and he finds himself in seminary years later with the understanding and frequently with the financial support of his wife. Sometimes a mature man with a successful career comes into the ministry because of the insight and perception of his own pastor...I know of more than one man who in the middle life has begun thinking toward the ministry because some tragic occurrence in his family was met with love and compassion by the local pastor.[8]

If this was so in 1958, it is even more so today. Yet, strangely, you may hear of those who find the whole matter of "leaving a career to follow a call" a bit "irresponsible."

The truth is that some mistakenly believe that the new trend in older seminarians is out of sync with the history of the church. I think there is enough evidence, Biblical and historical, to suggest that they are wrong. It is true that a 37- year-old seminarian was not

---

[8] We Have This Ministry, Robert N. Rodenmayer (New York: Harper & Brothers, 1959), 18,19.

the norm for the last several hundred years but, there have always been men who have been called from a prior career to the work of the Lord. In fact, the Bible is replete with such models.

ABRAHAM

Genesis 12.1 records the call of Abraham:

> "Now the LORD had said to Abram:
> 'Get out of your country
> From your family
> and from your father's house,
> To a land that I will show you...'"

When President George Bush was nominated by his party to head up the Republican ticket in 1990, he said in his acceptance speech:

> "...I know what it is to make a payroll..."

He was saying that he could identify with the millions of business owners and small family businesses across America in the responsibilities and accompanying pressures of providing for not only one's own family, but also in ensuring that one's employees were taken care of. In doing so, he was appealing to his experience as a rationale for leadership.

It is a valid assertion. God also uses men and women who have been given experience in such matters to build a dossier for Christian service.

In verse four, the Bible tells us that Abram was seventy-five years old. Not exactly a college sophomore! God called an older man from a well-settled life and sent him to establish a new nation. In Abraham God had a man with experience, experience in dealing with people, with managing the affairs of his large household (Gen. 12.5) and in the ebb and flow of day to day life. God had waited until Abram was well qualified for a divine task of raising up a new nation before He called him. Of course, Abram made mistakes, but they were generally mistakes of character (Gen. 16 and the "Hagar" incident; Gen. 20 and his lack of faith and lie about Sarah to Abimelech). His experiences stood him in good stead, but God still had to sanctify Abram to the work wherein he was called.

God has always called older men to the ministry. There are some tasks in God's plan that require experience in life that younger men simply cannot handle. It doesn't necessarily mean that they have it all together in terms of holiness any more than a younger man does. God will always sanctify us and perfect us as we follow Him. There are always areas in our lives to clean up. The example of Abraham, though, does underscore the fact that God has moved and still moves willing and faithful men from one vocation to another.

Maybe you are reading this now and saying to yourself,

> "I thought I was too old to serve God. I sense that the Lord is calling me, through His quiet urgings in my own life and through the comments of others, to preach the Gospel and shepherd His flock, but I thought that was just for younger men."

I hope you see through the example of God's dealing with Abraham, that there are simply some jobs in God's kingdom that require a more experienced man or woman. You may be that person. The story of theological education today is filled with people like you.

MOSES

A prince in the court of Egyptian royalty, educated in the finest schools of his day, filled with youthfulness and a life of possible usefulness to God, Moses would have been the perfect choice for seminary and the ministry during those early days. But God had to perfect a work in Moses. Once Moses committed an act of vengeance upon an Egyptian (Exodus 2.11,12; Acts 7.24,25). That act of passion cost Moses any opportunity for leadership among his own people (Exodus 2.14), and he went into exile in Midian. There for forty years this once proud man with a whole life of service to God before him lived with only what could-have been. He learned to be content with the life of a common herdsman. He learned the importance of family life. He was taught the lessons of the wilderness.

It was to that man, then, that God called. Burning bushes often appear in wilderness experiences to men who have been put on the shelf by this world.

> "Moses, Moses!"

> "Here I am."

Moses answered God. But when God told Moses what He had in mind—to lead the very people from whom Moses had fled—even Moses felt that God had the wrong man:

> "Who am I that I should go to Pharaoh, and I should bring the children of Israel out of Egypt?" (Ex.3.11)

Moses had a point, right? A royal rebel who had lost the trust of his own kinsmen (Ex. 2.14) and the favor of the court from which he came, Moses did not think he was a good "ministerial candidate." He was an aging man with a resume' that included a major identity crisis, manslaughter, and forty years of tending livestock in a two-bit desolate wilderness location.

But even through Moses' act of youthful passion and years of isolation, God was building a leader. God would call a man who had learned humility, a man who knew the depths of human depravity and God's grace, a man who knew how to herd a wayward flock in a dangerous wilderness, a man who knew that family wealth was more than mere palaces and jewels, a man who walked with God in the loneliness of his exile.

Burning bushes come to men like that. Vocations are initiated in the most unlikely of places and to the most unlikely of candidates.

There are some of you reading this example of Moses who are being called by God to the ordained ministry. Like Moses, you want to say, "Who am I to go...?"

You look back on your "wasted" years of youth and think, "Sure, I could have yielded my life to Christ then and could possibly have been a good seminary student and a useful minister of the Gospel, but that time is past. I'm 40 years old with a wife and children. I'm well into my career and feel fortunate just to have a job after all I've been through. God calling me?"

and God replies to those whom He is calling,

> "I will certainly be with you." (Exodus 3.12)

You see, burning bushes do indeed appear to those who are "could-have-beens." God calls men who "messed up" in their earlier years. God even calls them back to the place where they messed up. God uses men who have learned patience through waiting, who have cultivated a closeness to God through isolation from their past, and who have tended flocks in the "back of the desert (Ex.3.1)."

Is that you, dear friend? God has always called such people to his fields of service. Your exile has been your prayer closet. Your wilderness has been your academy. Your secular work has become your sacred witness. You have been under the sovereign hand of Almighty God and didn't even know it. Like Moses, you are possibly God's man for God's time for God's people.

No young man could have faced a royal court and led a rebellious people through a wilderness to their Promised Land. Only Moses could have done that. Maybe, you are God's man for God's time for God's people. If He is calling you—you can be sure that you are. and you can be sure that He who calls you will be faithful to equip you and sustain you.

THE DISCIPLES

If the lives of the Old Testament saints who were called to the "ordained ministry" are not enough to convince you that the older seminarian is nothing new, consider the lives of the New Testament saints. Consider the disciples of Jesus Christ.

In Mark 1.16-20 and Luke 5.2-11 we have the record of the vocational transition of four men: Simon (who was later called Peter), his brother, Andrew, and James and John the sons of Zebedee. As is well known, these men were fishermen. Their transition from professional fishermen and employers (note that they left their business to their employees in verse 20) to ministers of the Gospel of Christ is a further testimony to the way God prepares leaders.

There are several important observations which might be made at this point and which could be of some help to those of you considering a call to ministry:

1. Christ called them while they were faithfully discharging their duties. In Mark 1.1 it reads that "...as He walked by the sea of Galilee, He saw Simon and Andrew his brother casting a net into the sea; for they were fishermen." Simon and Andrew were not monastics waiting on a call. They were not "scholars-in-waiting" preparing for usefulness in God's kingdom by laying out a strategy for being selected for service. There is nothing

wrong with that, of course, and I highly recommend that young men and women who have been identified as candidates for the ministry or for missionary service by their local church leaders, begin to prepare for a life of service to Christ. I am simply saying that God calls some men and women, according to His Word, who are busy at their first careers, to leave those careers and follow Him. You are not disqualified from full-time service to God if your prior education was in preparation for business or a trade. To the contrary.

2. Christ used the disciples' former occupation as a metaphor for service in His kingdom's work. They were fishermen. He told them "Follow Me, and I will make you become fishers of men." So, their "first careers" were not just written off as wasted time and wasted energy. Their former professions became a living metaphor for service to Christ and His flock. In my own case I had been a salesman and later a sales manager as well as a business manager. I remember , in fact, a night I spent tossing and turning in bed. My wife, Mae, told me, "Honey, you're a salesman. But, God is just showing you that He has a greater product for you to sell." Well, some theologians may balk at my lovely wife's remark as demeaning to either the work of the pastor or to the solemnity of the call, but it hit home for me. Her remark validated my work as a salesman and showed me that God had been using my time in secular work to prepare me for sacred work. My lessons in sales—like the disciple's lessons in fishing—would be put to use by the Lord. Later, my training and experience in management would be put to use in the ministry. I am convinced from God's Word that whether one is a plumber or a salesman or a homemaker or a politician or a farmer, the skills acquired in that first profession are directly transferable to the work of ministry. Your time is not wasted. Jesus meets us on the job, validates our professions and experiences, and employs them for His own blessed designs. God does not, in fact, call all men from the boats. He called only four of them from such on that day when He walked by the Sea of Galilee. Today, He is walking in your office and in your factory. He is not calling all of those men and women to leave their work. But, He may be calling you. If He is—the Lord will transfer your skills, your tools, your experiences and even your failures into meaningful metaphors for Gospel service.

3. The fishermen left their businesses to become full-time workers for Christ. In verse 18 it reads that "They immediately left their nets and followed Him." Now, not all people are called to do this. I was—and I think many are. It would have been possible, as it was for many who encountered Christ, to follow Him without doing so "full-time." But Simon and Andrew and James and John were called to leave their first professions to become full-time laborers with the Savior. There comes a time when one must leave to go to seminary, to leave to prepare for a life of service to Christ and to His flock. Especially for those who are called to the pastorate or to the mission field, the vocation carries with it a requirement to transition from one's former profession to a new one. I am not saying that one cannot work while in seminary, or that, like St. Paul, one might have to "tent-make" to do ministry, but that the overarching focus of one's life becomes Word and Sacrament or Evangelism or Teaching, not fishing, mending tents, or baking bread. Now, that is a hard step to take. It is admittedly frightening to contemplate leaving a career to follow a call, but if Christ is calling, there is no choice. You will never be happy until you follow Him. He will lead and feed you along the way. The journey from the fishing boats to the seminary to the parish is filled with serendipitous moments of watching God do miracles. He supplies every need. He, in fact, uses your journey to erect a strong testimony to His faithfulness in your life that you will later share with others.

> "Blessed be the God and Father of our Lord Jesus Christ, the Father of mercies and God of all comfort, who comforts us in all our tribulation, that we may be able to comfort those who are in any trouble, with the comfort with which we ourselves are comforted by God.... For all of the promises of God in Him are Yes and in Him Amen, to the glory of God in Christ." (2 Cor. 2.3-4; 20).

4. Note also, in Mark 1.18 that the disciples who followed Jesus left "immediately." This is a very serious matter for those called of God. I almost lost my witness at my former vocation because I tried to stay too long. Why? I was sinfully fearful that God wouldn't take care of my family if I left to follow His call. It's called "Faithlessness," and I had a big case of it. You can't serve God and the world and the flesh at the same time. If God is calling you to the ministry, then be sensible and a good steward

of the things entrusted to you on the job, but at the same time, don't tarry. Do what God is calling you to do. It will be better for all.

OUR LORD JESUS CHRIST

Of course Jesus of Nazareth is our supreme example of the point we argue. Our Lord's own vocational transition is a model for those of us who didn't go to seminary at age twenty-one.

Jesus was a carpenter before He was a preacher. Because He grew in grace with God and man, I would imagine He was—no doubt like Joseph before Him—a renowned craftsman. What ministry skills He must have learned as He studied the grains of wood that he planed, the instruments that He depended on, the grumbling customers that He served and the satisfaction He enjoyed after completing a project! Jesus was thirty years of age before He would open up and read the lection from Isaiah at the synagogue. He was no longer a boy. He was in His second career: A carpenter-preacher.

As you read this, you may be on your lunch break in a carpentry shop and wondering that if God really is calling you to the ministry, how could He ever use a simple carpenter? Look at your hammer and your auger and your plum line: these were the primary tools of your Lord, who was the greatest preacher. Whether you labor now in a carpenter shop or a meat market or on the floor of Wall Street—be thankful if God has called you to preach, and be assured: you are laboring in a holy place. From such places future sermons, counseling sessions and outreach campaigns begin.

ISSUES

PROBLEMS AND POSSIBILITES FOR THE SECOND CAREER MINISTERIAL CANDIDATE

Now, while we must admit that the Word of God and God's acts in history confirm our proposition that God calls men in riper years, there are certain challenges associated with this fact.

ECONOMICS

The first difficulty with men called from a first career to the ministry is economic in nature. Usually men at this point have a family and a mortgage. The God who requires that we give priority to our families and their needs in this life never violates one of His commandments by issuing another, such as a call to ministry. If you are called to preach the Gospel, my friend, you must do so and take care of your family as you do. This is not impossible, but it is a tremendous undertaking that will call on your resourcefulness and dedication to both your family and your vocation.

When God called me to preach, I had a wife, a teenage daughter and a 93-year-old aunt to care for. God, of course, knew this when He called me, so when I prayed that He take care of my problem, He gave me a job. I had left home and career and friends to go off and prepare for a life of preaching. Many of you who read this would do the same, and so many before us have. The Lord promises that for those who are called to follow Him at personal expense, He will "repay" your losses and more in this life and the next.

I'll never forget the day I told my boss that I was leaving to go to seminary. He (an unbeliever) told me, "Well, I can't say I understand it, but it does seem a natural thing for you to do." Then, he said, "O.K., Mike, what can we do to help you? Will you need a job?" I thought I was going to drop right there. After regaining my composure, I replied, "I guess...why...yes! Of course!" The next day he called me and said, "I think this God of yours must be on your side. It looks like the man who hired you into the company 8 years ago is now the regional manager over the Southeast. I told him that you were going to go to seminary in Florida. He has a job opening for a salesman in Miami and it's yours if you want it."

In just a few days, we were on our way to South Florida and to Knox Seminary, and to my new job. God honored His Word as we yielded to Him. I have never experienced the power of God more than at those times in our lives.

So go ahead and face it: it's going to take money, and God has all the money in the world. Pray for a job, and anticipate God to open the door. Furthermore, treat your seminary experience as a mission, because it is. Ask your church leadership to help represent your needs to the congregation.

Then wait. God is about to move to provide your every need according to His riches in glory (Philippians 4.19).

FAMILY

I worked full-time and carried out an internship even as I went to school full time. I don't recommend that for everyone, but it can be done. I admit that there was little free time and plenty of rushed breakfasts and late nights, but, with the cooperation of the whole family, this short-term mission can be carried out.

I owe my wife, Mae, a great debt for managing our lives during those seminary years. There is no doubt that you, too, will need not only divine assistance, but wifely assistance as well.

My wife and I were very intentional about family time during those years (and still are!). For Mae and me Saturday mornings were sacred. We would go for a walk and then go to a mall and walk around together. Sometimes we might picnic. Sometimes we snuggled as we went up and down the aisles of Wal-Mart. It was our seminarian's Sabbath.

Make sure you plan for family.

HEALTH

The work of ministry is physically rigorous. It's more than carrying heavy textbooks that gets you, though! The task of going to seminary, working a job, caring for family life, and possibly even maintaining a yard, can suck away strength.

I recommend a thorough physical prior to coming to seminary. God is not asking you to ruin your health. If you're not up to it, you may want to re-think how you can pull off seminary.

For the average middle aged man (and woman) it is manageable, but we must also consider our health as we count the cost of service to Christ.

THE BENEFITS FOR THE OLDER SEMINARIAN

There are benefits that the older seminarian brings to his studies.

He is, first, generally more disciplined in scheduling. Schedules and time management issues are big in the lives of seminarians. Most of us have had work, studies, and ecclesiastical responsibilities thrown into the normal family requirements (which must never be subjugated to any other category).

The older seminarian also is, for the most part, more serious about his studies than the younger seminarians right out of undergraduate school.

Dr. Laura Schlesinger, Ph.D., is, of course, the popular host of a live, national radio call-in show. I rarely get the opportunity to listen to her, but the other day I happened to tune in at lunchtime to hear of a pathetic situation. A father had called to lament the downward cycle in his daughter's life. He had paid for her college and she had flunked out. She had since incurred a tremendous debt and was planning to move back in with her parents, so the father wanted to know if he should pay her way back to college for a "second" try! I was glad to hear the radio psychologist agree with me, that such a proposal was a ludicrous idea! The father's course of action revealed love confused with indulgence which would be a sure-fire method for enabling and perpetuating the girl's irresponsibility.

The older seminarian rarely exhibits behavior like that daughter; of course, few younger seminarians exhibit such lackadaisical behavior toward their studies. Nevertheless, the older student, generally exhibits a greater commitment to his work than the younger student because he has sacrificed so much simply to be in seminary. There is no daddy waiting in the wings to pull him out if he bombs. The older seminarian has generally learned such hard lessons earlier in his first career.

It is true, also, that the older seminarian brings life experiences with him to his new endeavor. Experience provides metaphors for dealing with the challenges that pop up in seminary. The seminarian with the most "metaphors" wins, so to speak. The daily grind of a career in business or a trade along with the possible years of marriage and childrearing are experiences that will stand the seminarian in good stead.

We have said nothing of the benefit that the older seminarian brings to both the theological institution and the Church itself. The older seminarian usually possesses skills and training in dealing with people and problems in an organization that is invaluable to the Church. Indeed, it could take years and several parish assignments to round out a younger minister.

THE POSSIBILITY BEFORE YOU

So, if you are feeling a little odd about the prospect of going to seminary, stop and consider that the Biblical model of ministers is quite a bit different than what developed in the Church years later. Consider, also, that you possess skills and experiences that will benefit both you and the Church of our Lord Jesus Christ.

A good friend of mine was once a disgruntled real estate salesman. He wasn't disgruntled because he wasn't successful, but rather, because he was lacking the completion in his life that could only be termed surrender to "The Call." After some years of transition (and sacrifice) he now leads an international missions program. When he and his wife made the decision to "leave a career to follow the Call" they termed their decision "The Great Adventure."

Truly it is.

Offer your life, now, as a living sacrifice to Jesus Christ and prepare for a great adventure of your own.

5

RESPONSE

A THEOLOGY OF DECISION-MAKING BEFORE MAKING A CHANGE TO GO INTO THE MINISTRY

You've read the previous chapter, I trust. You've done a little Bible study on your own, I hope. It may be that you left a marker at this point and decided to seek some Godly counsel before moving on. Good.

I hope you see that a mid-career transition into the ordained ministry is not historically or Biblically odd. It is, rather, the norm. I hope you can appreciate—even if you are not called to the ministry—that the rise in the median age at graduate schools of theology is not an anomaly. It is reflective of God working in the souls of His people who are increasingly abandoning other pursuits to heed the call of Christ when He says, "...The harvest truly is plentiful, but the laborers are few. Therefore pray the Lord of the harvest to send out laborers into His harvest."[9]

GO BACK TO YOUR HOME AND TELL OTHERS: WHEN GOD SAYS 'NO' TO THE ORDAINED MINISTRY

Now, however, you are faced with the weighty matter of putting legs on your theology. If you are not called, you must return to your field with a renewed sense of purpose. You must return to your home church with zeal to serve Christ in those several and sundry ministry opportunities there. Consider a model case in the Bible:

> and when He got into the boat, he who had been demon-possessed begged Him that he might be with Him. However, Jesus did not permit him, but said to him, "Go home to your friends, and tell them what great things the Lord has done for you, and how He has had compassion on you."

---

[9] Matthew 9.37,38

> and he departed and began to proclaim in Decapolis
> all that Jesus had done for him; and all marveled.
> (Mark 5.18-20, NKJV)

We have here a man, the Gadarene demoniac, who had been healed and transformed by Christ. His response? To leave his environment and follow Him in humble service. Jesus responded with a "no." Instead, He called this passionate, grateful fellow to remain with family and friends and neighbors and share the compassion of the Lord with them. The healed demoniac did just that. and "all marveled." This is the message to the one who has been told "No, my son" to the Ordained Ministry.

You must see yourself, then, as a person of worth and value before God. That is potentially very difficult. We have the tendency, at such times and in such cases, to think that our ministry is somehow of less use to God. Of course the transformed demoniac was not to be one of the twelve, but he had a powerful ministry "in Decapolis."

Consider, also, the clear teaching of St. Paul:

> For as we have many members in one body, but all the members do not have the same function, so we, being many, are one body in Christ, and individually members of one another. Having then gifts differing according to the grace that is given to us, let us use them: if prophecy, let us prophesy in proportion to our faith; or ministry, let us use it in our ministering; he who teaches, in teaching; he who exhorts, in exhortation; he who gives, with liberality; he who leads, with diligence; he who shows mercy, with cheerfulness. (Romans 12.4-8, NKJV).

The Apostle speaks of "gifts differing according to the grace that is given to us..." He then lists several - but, surely, not all gifts. The weighty matter for you, now, is to consider your passion, your experience, and your service to Jesus Christ and to His people. The outcome of those considerations will become the gifts of God through your life to us: the Church.

If you are one who has listened for the voice of the Lord and have heard "No, my child" to the ordained ministry; then, you will soon hear "This way, my little one." As Eli instructed Samuel, "Go...if He calls you...say, 'Speak, Lord, for Your servant hears.'"[10]

May you hear your name spoken clearly. "It is the Lord. Let Him do what seems good to Him."[11]

May you serve joyfully.

THE PATHWAY: WHEN GOD SAYS "YES," GOD SAYS "GO"

I address my remarks, now, for those of you who, like Samuel, have heard the Lord and believe with Paul that "Woe is me" if you do not follow Christ as an ordained minister. For you, too, we must repeat the admonition of Eli:

> It is the Lord. Let Him do what seems good to Him.[13]

You must now survey the road ahead. You must now count the cost of obedience. If God has called you to the Ordained Ministry—as best as you can determine through the process described previously—then, it is, indeed, time to begin the process...and it is a process, as we shall see.

Before I go further, I want to take what I suspect is a very necessary diversion to a different but related matter.

Spiritual landmines are placed, it seems, at every turn in the process of leaving a career to follow a call. Probably the first one you will encounter is set by your own self-interests, and the potentially disabling instrument is nestled deep in your own soul.

URGENCY: "LET THE DEAD BURY THE DEAD" OR WHY IT IS BEST TO GET ON WITH IT

What is the landmine? It's the matter of "putting it off." For many at this point, this will be a familiar response. Not a small number of older seminarians are making a mid-career transition because they

---

[10] 1 Samuel 3.9.

[11] 1 Samuel 3.18.

[12] 1 Samuel 3.18.

[13] Ibid.

refused to act on God's call to them earlier in life. Thus, when they face the matter once more, they must face the same old "demons." What are you to do?

Plain and simple: if you are called, waste no time. Get on with it.

Yes, I know you have responsibilities at your company or organization. We'll get into that later. Yes, I know you have a family. God knows that and is already dealing with the souls of your precious loved ones if He is calling you. In fact, many times, they knew it before you did!

Yes, I know you don't have all of your bills paid off and you wanted to wait to go to seminary after you were in better financial shape. Yes, I know...and God knows.

But, the fact is this: either you are called to the ordained ministry or you are not. If you are called—and you have worked through that process of identifying the outer and inner call and have sought counsel from others who have encouraged you in this —then, you must simply go.

The matter before you is the matter of urgency.

I know about all of these things because I was there. I knew I was called to the ministry. My wife knew I was called. The problem was, I was locating each and every reason why I should not go to seminary and was offering them up to God, hoping He would buy it.

He didn't.

I was making a sales call, as I remember, in Dublin, Ohio. I was in my rental car and, as usual, had tuned in to find a local Christian radio station. Hoping to hear some soothing music to quiet my troubled soul at that time (troubled, again, over the matter of when to go and how to do it), I could find only a preacher. "As it happened" (a favorite introduction in the Scriptures to pivotal events), the minister—a local preacher— was preaching on Luke 9 and a very familiar Scripture:

> Now it happened as they journeyed on the road, that someone said to Him, "Lord, I will follow you wherever You go." and Jesus said to him, "Foxes have holes and birds of the air have nests, but the Son of Man has nowhere to lay His head." Then He

> said to another, "Follow Me." But he said, "Lord, let me first go and bury my father." Jesus said to him, "Let the dead bury their own dead, but you go and preach the kingdom of God." and another also said, "Lord, I will follow You, but let me first go and bid them farewell who are at my house." But Jesus said to him, "No one, having put his hand to the plow, and looking back, is fit for the kingdom of God." After these things the Lord appointed seventy others also, and sent them two by two before His face into every city and place where He Himself was about to go. Then He said to them, "The harvest truly is great, but the laborers are few; therefore pray the Lord of the harvest to send out laborers into His harvest." (Luke 9.57-10.2).[14]

For me, that passage became the power of the Spirit to change my life.

In the story Jesus issues a call for laborers to go out into the harvest and proclaim the Kingdom of God in Christ. There is urgency resounding in the whole text. The Lord, knowing the heart of mankind,[15] reminded his eager followers about the cost of service. There is an uncertainty to the ministry and a built-in opposition to it in this age that can potentially even render you without a home or a pillow! This is the cost of accepting this call. Yet, if you are compelled by a call resounding even unto the deepest parts of your soul, then you must respond—also at great cost —to the Lord of the Harvest.

The problem with one of them is that he is "not quite ready." He has to go and bury his father. The great New Testament scholar, A.T. Robertson, handles it this way:

> The burial of one's father was a sacred duty (Gen. 25.9), but, as in the case of Tobit 4:3, this scribe's father probably was still alive. What the scribe apparently meant was that he could not leave his

---

[14] See also Matthew 8.19-22.

[15] "But Jesus did not commit Himself to them, because He knew all men, and had no need that anyone should testify of man, for He knew what was in man." (John 2.24,25)

> father while still alive to follow Jesus around over the country...The explanation is that the spiritually dead can bury the literally dead...The harshness of this proverb to the scribe probably is due to the fact that he was manifestly using his aged father as an excuse for not giving Christ active service. But go thou and publish abroad the kingdom of God. The scribe's duty is put sharply...Christ called him to preach, and he was using pious phrases about his father as a pretext. Many a preacher has had to face a similar delicate problem of duty to father, mother, brothers, sisters and the call to preach. This was a clear case. Jesus will help any man called to preach to see his duty. Certainly Jesus does not advocate renunciation of family duties on the part of preachers.[16]

Th radio preacher didn't put it quite like old Dr. Robertson, but he interpreted it in precisely the same spirit.

The message hit me like a brick.

I pulled my rental car over the side of the interstate highway. "Lord, you got me." I knew the man in the passage was none other than myself, and I knew the Lord of the Harvest was making it ever so clear:

> "I have called you. Go. Now. I know you have other responsibilities. Take care of them. I'll help. But, don't use them as excuses. Let the dead bury the dead—but you follow me."

When I returned home, I told my wife and I committed to leave all and follow the call. As it turned out, it took one more year, but that was God's business—not mine. There were several issues that had to be resolved, and God took them firmly in hand to do. I had committed and He would take care of the rest.

I never experienced greater peace than I did during those days.

---

[16] *Word Pictures in the New Testament*, Volume II, "The Gospel According to Luke," Archibald Thomas Robertson (New York: Harper and Brothers Publishers, 1930), 141.

So, if you are called, then yield your life to the Lord and get ready. God is about to do some wonderful things in your life.

DECENCY AND ORDER: THE RULING MOTIF IN THE PROCESS OF ACCEPTING THE CALL

Once you commit to follow the call, you've got to get a few things straight:

One—Your call originated from God...yes...BUT...

Two—It was given to you through the Church (The "Outer" Call) and must be validated through the Church ("counseling" from your pastor and lay leadership and, possibly, a "middle judicatory" such as a presbytery, diocese, association, or district) and must be supervised by the Church.

The same Apostle Paul who started his epistles with underscoring the divine nature of his call[17] is the Apostle Paul who was—after his calling—brought by Barnabas to the other apostles:

> and he [Barnabas] declared to them how he had seen the Lord on the road, and that He had spoken to him, and how he had preached boldly at Damascus in the Name of Jesus. (Acts 9.27).

This is a vitally important point for you to make right now. Your calling must be from God, but that will not allow one to act independently of God's Church. Like Paul, our gifts and our calling and the practice of our ministry is under the oversight of the Church. There should be no "loose cannons" in the Church. Order and decency—so vital in worship—is necessary to bring up at this point.

---

[17] Note Paul's constant appeal to his divine call: "...through the will of God..." in 1 Corinthians 1.1; "...by the will of God..." in 2 Corinthians 1.1; most pointedly in Galatians 1.1, "Paul, an apostle (not from men nor through man, but through Jesus Christ and God the Father who raised Him from the dead)..."; "by the will of God" in Ephesians 1.1; "...by the will of God..." in Colossians 1.1; "...by the commandment of God our Savior and the Lord Jesus Christ, our hope..." in Philippians 1.1 and "I thank Christ Jesus our Lord who has enabled me, because He counted me faithful, putting me into the ministry..." in Philippians 1.12; "...by the will of God..." in 2 Timothy 1.1.

WHAT NOW?

The answer, very simply, to that question will be provided, usually, by the Church. Again, a great deal of the particulars depends upon the denomination. Yet, there are a number of similarities. Whether you must have an undergraduate degree, or a certain number of Humanities within a given undergraduate program, whether you will have to go to a graduate school of theology or a Bible school or "pastor's school" depends on your church affiliation. Refer to your pastor and to your denomination. I would like you, though, to consider some fundamental values in the process.

1. If the Call is so great...shouldn't the preparation be equal to the Vocation?

I happen to believe that the answer to that is self-evident. The call to ordained ministry is great. It is, really, a gift. God is the giver, and the call to preach means there is a resident gift of preaching along with other gifts. Thus, unto whom much is given much is required.[18]

I remember thinking when God called me that if He were to give me 30 years of ministry (and at my age, then, that was a reasonable possibility), my commitment to invest three good years in preparation would be simply my "tithe" to God for the gift of ministry He had given to me. I determined, then, that I would seek the very best academic and practical training I could get in order to prepare for the Gospel ministry.

Now, I submit another question:

2. How Do You Leave Your Career and Maintain Your Witness to Christ?

You are called to the ordained ministry. You are also, probably, a successful salesman, manager, teacher, computer programmer, or craftsman. So, how do you make the move with integrity?

I almost tripped at this point. I don't want you to.

---

[18] "For everyone to whom much is given, from him much will be required; and to whom much has been committed, of him they will ask the more." (Luke 12.48b)

The next chapter will seek to help you make the transition from a career to your call.

6

TRANSITION

PREPARING FOR THE CALL

There is an art to "leaving." Shakespeare, writing in Macbeth, made this observation:

"Nothing in his life
Became him like the leaving it; he died
As one that had been studied in his death
To throw away the dearest thing he ow'd
As 'twere a careless trifle."[19]

While this is said of one who left this world for eternity, may it be said of those who leave a career to follow God's call.

HOW TO LEAVE YOUR CAREER WITH INTEGRITY

The issue is very relevant to the pursuit of the call. First, your leaving is a testimony to God's activity in your life. The way you handle it will speak to others about the reality of God! If you handle it poorly, many will assume that the whole business of ministry and "church" is a sham—something less committed to excellence that the marketplace. Alternatively, if you "leave well," they just may get interested in this God who calls.

As I related at the end of last chapter: I came close to tripping at this juncture.

I was waiting too long. I was dealing with the "let the dead bury the dead" issues and meanwhile allowing the complicated emotional charges (and all which that entails) to detonate at work. In short while doing a great deal of pre-seminary study and reading, I wasn't giving everything I could on the job. Furthermore, I knew that at some time I would leave and therefore was "letting up" without realizing it.

---

[19] I, iv, 7.

Now, I am not advocating irresponsible behavior at this point. Prior to seminary, particularly those with family, one must do everything possible to secure income and take care of the needs of your family—as well as tuition. What I am advocating, is this: if God has called you, don't ride on the back of your employer too long. Let them know. Be forthright. Don't sneak around. Develop a plan and watch God do the rest.

Now many of your co-workers and friends and well-meaning relatives will tell you that you are crazy. If in fact you are highly successful in your present career, this fact only adds to their suspicion that you are crazy. "Why are you throwing it all away? Can't you serve God at the Firm?" Well, yes. We dealt with that earlier in the theology of vocation. But, you have been called to the ministry of Word and Sacrament. You will have to be patient with them. It probably took several years for God to get through to you, so be as longsuffering with others as God was with you! Most of them will come around. Some of them will even come to faith in Christ in all of this. Others, probably a minority, will sulk about this for a long, long time. Why? Because your decision to leave a career—a successful career—and follow a call, strikes at their decision—probably many years earlier—NOT to do it. You are living out their forfeited dreams. Secretly, even they will respect you. Pray for them. Love them. Treat them the way God treated you, with mercy and grace.

Its time to go and prepare for your call.

CHOOSING A SEMINARY

There are over 65,000 seminary students enrolled in 237 accredited graduate schools of theology in North America.[20] Of that number, 50.15% are over 35 years of age.[21] Better than 40% are under 35 years of age,[22] but even at age 30, they, along with the majority of seminarians, have left a career to follow the call to ministry. Clearly, if you have a concern about being the only "older student" in the

---

[20] The Association of Theological Schools in the United States and Canada Fact Book, 1997, pages 40-43.

[21] Ibid.

[22] Ibid.

class, your concern is misplaced. Most seminarians fall into your category. Most students have "left a career to follow a call."

Before going too deeply into the selection of a seminary, you should consider your denomination's requirements, as well as your local judicatory. Some associations, presbyteries, districts, and dioceses allow their candidates to go to seminaries outside of their jurisdiction (and increasingly, outside of their theological tradition). So discuss the options with your denominational representative prior to going any further.

Once you've got that information in hand, there are several criteria that I would suggest you use in your evaluation:

1. DOCTRINAL INTEGRITY

Choose a seminary that is faithful to the message God has called you to proclaim. This doesn't mean, of course, that you should not be challenged in your beliefs or have your horizons broadened as to what other's believe. You should be. Yet, it is equally clear that if you are a Calvinist and choose to go to Asbury Theological Seminary because you happen to live in Wilmore, Kentucky, you will undergo extreme theological discomfort (since Asbury, a very fine Wesleyan school is decidedly NOT Calvinistic!). The same would be true for a convinced Wesleyan who wanted to serve in the Church of the Nazarene and decided to attend Reformed Theological Seminary. Now, each of these would get a superior theological education, to be sure, but within the context of "competing" traditions. Unless you are convinced that God is calling you to "test" your convictions, I would advise attending a graduate school that has some theological proximity to your own basic convictions.

2. FACULTY COMMITMENT

As one who has led a seminary, taught, counseled and recruited seminary students, I have often stated that if I had a Godly, thoroughly committed, and highly student-driven faculty, I could start a seminary in a Holiday Inn and "they would come."

Your choice of a seminary to prepare you for the ministry must include a thorough examination of the faculty. Your professors are your mentors. Your concept of God, of the Church, of your role in the ministry is, to a great degree, derived from the vision and commitment of the faculty under whom you train.

I would look for a commitment to the Scriptures and to a commitment to the historic, classical confessions of the Church. You, of course, can locate that easily enough in the institutional mission statement. The proof in the pudding, though, will be in the individual commitment of the professors.

How do you make such a determination? You would read their publications (which is also a gauge of their passion for the Faith), you would talk to former students, and you would conduct a formal interview with them, if possible. If you are told that a given professor has published so and so number of academic articles, ask for more information, say, for instance, "Has he ever pastored a congregation himself?"

When God called me to preach, my wife and I, determined that we would go to the best school possible in order to prepare us for a life of preaching and service in the Church. We felt the Call demanded such a commitment on our part. Our decision to attend a seminary that was just beginning[23] was largely made by our personal interviews with the professors. Again, I don't advise choosing a graduate school of theology based upon the age of the ivy on the brick but by the relationship of the Seminary to the Vine. Jesus said "I am the Vine and you are the branches. He who abides in Me, and I in him, bears much fruit; for without Me you can do nothing." (John 15.5)

3. PRAXIS AND ACADEMIC EXCELLENCE

Choose a school that combines academic excellence with a commitment to praxis—that is, practice. One without the other is no good. Over and over you will hear from preachers, "My seminary was academic—but not practical." Or, "My school relays stressed the practical, but I feel I didn't get an education."

"That which we have seen and heard we declare unto you" (1 John 1.3) is an important Scripture to meditate upon when considering a seminary. Have these professors, my prospective mentors, experienced the front line ministry to such a degree that they are

---

[23] Knox Theological Seminary, Fort Lauderdale, Florida in 1990.

able to integrate scholarship with praxis? Or, have strong reading and research informed the practical experience?

The question is not just "are they published," but "have they preached?" Demand both. It will stand you in good stead in the years ahead.

4. RESOURCES

The technical resources that most seminaries have prior to being accredited are self-evident (books, computers, etc.).

One of the greatest resources you could ever get, however, is not even on the seminary campus: I speak of the resource of being connected to local churches. This is THE resource link you want to look for. There should be strategic and synergistic relationships built between local churches and the seminary. In the local church you will get the spiritual and practical resources you need for you and for your family. In the local church you will get field opportunities. In the local church you can observe working sessions, vestries, councils and the like [In local churches, you will worship and work with those men and women—the laity— who will one day call you and who will, in your seminary days, keep your theological training in perspective].

5. JOB OPPORTUNITIES

Many seminaries keep strong relationships built with local employers. Ask about that. Few, however, can guarantee you a job. You've got to take the initiative. For a person who has left a career to follow a call, though, this ought to be pretty easy stuff. Some of the places you should not overlook in your search are: funeral homes (providing comfort to families and arranging funerals will be good experience), hotels and motels, and sales jobs (if you're up to it—these are great since they allow you to dart into a class then go back out into the field as needed).

HOW ABOUT DISTANCE LEARNING?

Distance learning essentially involves bringing the classroom to you. In seminaries that means taking graduate level seminary courses without having to leave your community.

A Description of Distance Learning in Seminaries

Central to all distance learning schemes is the delivery system. Typically, the delivery system for a distance learning course is video or audiotape or courses on the Internet. Many distance learning opportunities happen in your own home. There are others—I think the better ones—which are offered at central sites, (i.e., churches, libraries, rented facilities). These usually have on-site leaders.

Those Who Should Consider it

If you are unable to leave to go to seminary because of peculiar family circumstances, such as health, then, distance education is a great blessing for you. Even if you are intending to go the traditional route, you may want to investigate distance learning as a way to get started early. Many seminaries will allow you to earn up to 12 hours in distance learning formats prior to seminary.

Those Who Should Not

I firmly believe that while distance education is a great breakthrough for some, it is not for all. There are clear advantages of leaving to go to seminary. I want to discuss those now.

WHY YOU SHOULD CONSIDER A MOVE TO A SEMINARY CAMPUS

THE POWER OF LEAVING AND FOLLOWING

Despite the temptation to follow a distance learning approach, which is so popular and so available today, I would urge you to consider the dynamics of actually leaving to follow your call.

A minister of the Gospel is always called to "go." We are called to "go and make disciples." For most of us this means that we will not minister in our hometowns. Even our Lord said, "a prophet is without honor in his own country." Most ministers will serve several churches in addition to other sorts of ecclesiastical appointments. Most of those will require a move. Abraham moved. Moses moved. Jeremiah moved. Amos moved. Paul moved. Leaving to follow Christ in order to carry the Gospel to others generally requires moving. Now, it's not as bad as it is for some of our brothers in years past—like Methodists (who would move every two years or so)—but it's still part and parcel to the job.

So what am I getting at here? To leave and follow Christ in a "ministry of preparation"—the essence of seminary—is, for most of us, our first act of total submission to the Gospel call.

Whether it's across the state or across the nation (or globe, if you are so inclined), following the Lord and moving to the campus of the seminary is still an exercise in ministerial faithfulness.

THE CENTRIFUGAL EFFECT OF A MENTOR

Another great reason why one should go to seminary rather than experience it through the Internet is to get hold of the centrifugal effect of a good mentor. Let me explain.

A seminary professor differs from other professors. They are, almost universally, ordained ministers, themselves. Most will have had considerable years of parish work behind them. All of them at your choice of seminaries, I trust, will have been personally called by God to equip the Church by training her pastors. The vision of 2 Timothy 2.2 is burnished into the souls of most of them:

> and the things that you have heard from me among many witnesses commit these to faithful men who will be able to teach others also. (2 Timothy 2.2, NKJV).

The seminary professor is a mentor who instills vision into his students. Seminary is all about imparting a vision of God, of man, of Christ, of the Church, and of the power of the Gospel. We may apply the words of Joel's prophecy to the fruit of a good seminary professor's labor:

> You old men shall dream dreams, your young men shall see visions. (Joel 2.28).

Seminary should provide mentors who are like NASA rockets, they propel future ministers off into the unreached worlds with such a strong vision of God and His Plan that the vision—their rocket booster—will literally keep them moving forward for the rest of their lives.

The booster will fall away, but the ship will go through the initial difficult atmospheric years of early ministry, and through the unexpected trials of parish work, and to a faithful completion of one's mission.

That is why you must consider "leaving" for seminary. You simply need the boost.

The Benefit of Iron Sharpening Iron

Obviously, one of the main differences between doing seminary work on-line and in the classroom is interaction with others. You need interaction not only with teachers, but equally as important —with fellow students.

> As iron sharpens iron, So a man sharpens the countenance of his friend.[24]

You may be different in your make-up, but if God has called you to preach, then you are all mined out of the same cavern. Iron needs iron says the Word of God. You won't get iron, usually, over the Internet.

One arrives at seminary—and as this book is reflecting, they are increasingly coming from first careers—with all sorts of preconceived notions, expectations, and... fears. You enter your first class with those brewing thoughts and feelings and within one or two days you invariably get a dose of reality that upsets your romantic view of seminary.

The Benefit to the Family

For the family the physical move to a seminary can be—in the best cases—stressful; and in the worse cases—crushing. A good deal depends on your family situation. For many, though, the move to seminary is the pivotal event in family life that transforms a family into a pastoral family. A man can be an attorney and his wife may be only minimally involved with his day-to-day career. A person may be a sheet metal worker and his spouse be very distant from his work, but not so in the ministry. The wife and the children are intimately involved with the work of the minister of the Gospel and the sooner one learns that the better. Leaving to go to seminary is helpful in this regard.

Again for a healthy family, the transition out of your former life and to seminary is recommended and is very helpful in the process of surrendering to God's call.

---

[24] Proverbs 27.17.

In our family, we "tried" to move to seminary once and God stopped it. He stopped it because our daughter was not ready for it. She had some deep spiritual issues that had to be dealt with prior to our family going into the ministry. Did we know it at the time? Not completely, though we had an idea. We were disappointed at first, but God showed her the problem and there was significant healing. Once this was taken care of, the Lord cleared a path for us the following year.

If there are underlying spiritual issues that need addressing and that are not being dealt with in your family, ask God to show them to you and to bring healing before making any move. It is a good idea to solicit the observation of others who love you and who can help you come to terms with this vital subject.

THE BENEFIT TO YOUR FUTURE CHURCHES

Personally, I knew that I could never stand before a congregation and admonish them to step out in faith in God if I did not step out in faith to go to seminary. That conviction proved to be a good one. God met my needs along the way and taught me truths there that I could have never learned had I taken the safer route of staying at my home. The Church benefits, then, when her ministers have experienced the power of God firsthand. A minister who has left all to follow God—first at seminary—is a minister who has a story to tell about God's faithfulness. Show me such a minister and I will show you a congregation that is grateful that its minister "left his career to follow his call."

THE LIFE OF A SEMINARY FAMILY

I will never forget our lives at seminary. Was it hectic? Unmercifully. Was it fatiguing? Most certainly. Would I do it again? Without a doubt, I would. My wife and I can honestly say that our seminary years were some of the very best in our family life.

Contrary to some popularly held notions, seminary is not designed to break you, to discourage you, or to take your faith away from you! Seminary is a formation station. It should be a meaningful time for each member of the family and I firmly believe that it can be.

GETTING THERE

When we went to seminary, our family consisted of my wife, myself, our daughter who was a highschooler at the time, and my ninety one-year-old aunt who had reared me.

I will never forget the move there. My wife and daughter went first and moved in with the Dean of Faculty and his wife. In two weeks I packed up our home and made the 1,500 mile trip. My aunt remained behind at a nursing home until we could get moved in. Later, after we were settled (in about three weeks), my wife flew back to get my aunt, and the two of them returned.

Now, prior to our move, my wife and I had made a trip down to the seminary (which was in Fort Lauderdale). We secured a real estate representative who was recommended by the seminary. My wife told him our needs, and our budget, and the three of us spent a few days looking around (and even praying together about it). We found a perfect home for our needs.

I would definitely recommend taking that scouting trip to set up employment, housing, schooling, and to get a general feel for what will become your home for three to five years.

SETTLING IN

One of the most important steps in making a transition is to immediately find your "place." By that, I mean that each member of the family must begin to "fit in" to the new locale. This must be intentional. Someone is going to have to make it happen.

Now the circumstances themselves will be of help here. Seminary, work, school, church life, and ordinary household chores will begin to drive you towards settling in. For many seminarians today this process will not be unlike one of your transfers or a permanent change of duty station in the military. If you resist the process and give in to thinking about what "could have been" had you stayed in your career, you are on a sure pathway for unhappiness.

> Trust in the Lord with all your heart, and lean not on your own understanding; In all your ways acknowledge Him, and He shall direct your paths. (Proverbs 3.5,6, NKJV).

You need to settle in.

ROLES

Before we went to seminary I took great pride in my lawn and spent no small amount of time in cultivating it. With the advent of term papers, sermons to write, visits to make, and 2,000 pages a week reading, my ability to even mow the lawn was seriously impaired! So, my wife, formerly proprietor of the house only, became quite adept at gardening. In fact her running battle with the hedges in our south Florida rental became the stuff of family folklore. I even bought her an electric hedge trimmer for her birthday!

All of this is to say that at seminary, because of school and work and ministry training, old schedules, habits, and roles must be flexible. Now that seminary is well behind me (and post-graduate school after that), I am happy to say that I run the weed-eater once more. But there were necessary role exchanges "for the sake of the Gospel" during seminary.

Talk it out now and be ready, at least temporarily, to adjust your roles to meet the mission.

CHILDREN

We left for seminary with an eleventh grader. We were, thus, understandably concerned about the move. But as it turned out, God took care of our concerns—and our daughter. She flourished during those seminary years and even met her future husband while there.

God sent His own Son into a family and thus blessed that most basic of His human building instruments. We need to, throughout the process of call and response, affirm that institution and affirm the heritage of the Lord: our children.

I remember talking to the daughter of a restaurant owner who told me that running a restaurant is definitely a team sport! There were always dishes to wash, floors to clean, food to order, food to cook, and customers to wait on. The same is true of the ministry. It's a team sport, and the team is the family. Seminary is a ministry of preparation, and, so, going to seminary and giving the children an opportunity to make the schedule work is important. What they learn during that time will help them to transition, as you must, into the joys and challenges of parish life.

Another point: don't let them stop being children.

I once saw a little fellow on the playground who was the son of the Episcopal rector. I said to this little five-year-old who was playing with my own son, "Aren't you the Episcopal minister's son?" "No," he answered sharply, "I am my daddy's son!"

Yes, that is it all right. They are first and foremost children who need whatever other children need.

Furthermore, do not stop being a parent to them. Don't let seminary studies and the pursuit of a ministerial career spoil your children's childhood. If you fail at being a parent, you are washed up as a minister before you ever started. Or did you do that in your first career? Repent of it. God desires the hearts of the fathers to be turned to the children.[25] Encourage them in their own pursuits. Prioritize them. Be there for them. Involve them in your ministry, but don't put them on parade. Don't fall into the temptation of trying to create an image of the perfect pastoral family. It works for a while, but then it can get ugly when they get old enough to sense what's going on. Just be Dad. Let them just be children.

FINANCES

When we went off to school, I sold stocks, depleted savings, appealed to my home church for support, worked full-time and went to school full-time and even pulled off an internship that had a small stipend.

I needed every last penny of it.

Seminary costs and so does raising a family. It's great to pay off all of your bills before you go. If you can do that, fine. If your financial obligation has prevented you from going to seminary, then wrest yourself free. Your testimony is at stake. If, however, you have a reasonable debt, but want to wait until everything is perfect, I say to you: "let the dead bury the dead." It might be those finances and your desire to have everything just so have become an instrument of the Enemy to prevent you from being obedient. Like most of us, you probably will have to work and go to school at the same time. Actually, the combination can teach you a great deal about time management, so it's not all bad.

---

[25] Malachi 4.4,5 and Luke 1.17.

Obviously, if you are not budgeting, begin now. You'll need a financial system to get through. Remember to budget some time to get away for a family vacation and for weekly "retreats" for you and your spouse, if you are married. For Mae and me it meant a Saturday afternoon stroll in a suburban shopping mall and a couple of coffees. It cost about $3.00 per week, but the memories and the investment in the marriage remain priceless.

Since I am arguing for seminary as a ministry in itself, a ministry of preparation—a mission if there ever was one—I believe one of the best preliminary things you can do is to raise support for your ministry. Hopefully, your local church has encouraged you to do this and will want to stand with you during this time.

FRIENDS AND FELLOWSHIP

Seminary was one of our greatest experiences in our lives and most certainly in our marriage. Perhaps a primary reason that we feel that way is that we made and have retained deep friendships. Think about it: You all are there in the same place, have gone through the same experience of leaving a career to follow a call (even younger students have left the possibility of another career to be there), are desperately trying to memorize Hebrew verb forms! You can't have more in common than that!

If you are thinking that leaving a career means launching out without friends, forget it. God will provide you with deep, lasting friendships built upon a love for the Gospel and a common call to labor in His fields.

SPIRITUAL FORMATION

As our society transitioned from an agrarian-based society to an industrial society and then again, in our own day, to an information based society, we have had to make adjustments. Modernity hasn't always been kind to the soul. Churches have had to be intentional about ministries to the modern challenges we face.

There is a similar threat to the man and woman and family as they go into seminary. The demands of school, work, and family chores work together to potentially threaten our spirituality. Amazing as it may seem, seminarians are more prone to spiritual dryness and even decay, than the average committed Christian. Why? In short seminary poses a threat to balance. It will become possible for you to study the doctrine of the Holy Spirit and yet quench His power in your own life. How? By approaching the doctrine in a dry, academic, detached fashion. The motivation for your understanding of the Holy Spirit as He is revealed in Scripture is singular: To pass the upcoming examination. This is, of course, necessary. But far more important is your motivation to grow in "grace" as well as in "knowledge." The overriding motivation in your life remains: To follow Christ in the power of the Spirit.

It is true, also, that seminary life is similar to pastoral life. Those who handle holy things day in and day out are prone to treat their spiritual lives with an equally perfunctory spirit.

How do you avoid this trap of the ministry?

In a phase, the answer is this: "Go to the Mountain."

The Lord's greatest work seemed to be carried on before and after ministry on a mountain. Consider some of these passages:

> Now after six days Jesus took Peter, James, and John his brother, led them up on a high mountain by themselves; (Matthew 17.1, NKJV).

> Then the eleven disciples went away into Galilee, to the mountain which Jesus had appointed for them. (Matthew 28.16, NKJV).

> Now it came to pass in those days that He went out to the mountain to pray, and continued all night in prayer to God. (Luke 6.12, NKJV).

The mountain is the place where God is. The mountain in your life, seminarian or minister, is the place where others aren't looking, where professors aren't examining, where parishioners and peers are absent. It is the place where you and God meet and carry on your soul's unseen business. What happens there will affect everything else in your life and, consequently, your ministry.

Make daily and weekly appointments, then, to meet God on the mountain, or in the closet (Matthew 6.6), and explore your life with Him. Ask Him to show you His glory in your life and your work. Plead with Christ to examine the sinful motivations, sinful propensities, and sinful acts in your life. Ask the Lord to forgive you, to cleanse you, to renew you. Lift up others—especially those who trouble you in your life.[26]

Do this, and the mountain will transform the daily valley into a sanctuary.

---

[26] "But I say to you, love your enemies, bless those who curse you, do good to those who hate you, and pray for those who spitefully use you and persecute you." (Matthew 5.44, NKJV)

IDENTITY

ESSAYS ON BECOMING AND BEING A MINISTER

One of the greatest struggles you will have in leaving a career to follow a call is—identity. You were successful business people, lawyers, tradesmen, and teachers. Now, you are... what? You are a minister-in-training. Then, after that, you will become a Minister of the Gospel of Jesus Christ. There are roles and expectations (some Biblical and some just plain ridiculous, not to mention harmful) that others and we have of the ordained ministry. It is good to sit down for a while and consider them, now rather than later.

Many who fail to contemplate and work through these issues have, at some point in their ministry, a veritable identity crisis.

To better help you prepare for your "identity crisis," I draw your attention to several important topics which I trust will be of some help to you:

1. I will present some thoughts on "Why Young Men Do Not Go Into the Ministry," which will help, I pray, some of you work through past struggles and prepare you to provide some insight in vocational counseling in the future.

2. Then I will introduce the idea that seminary is not simply a place to learn, but a place to begin the ministry in "The Ministry of a Seminarian."

3. "What Color is Your Pulpit?" is intended to help you categorize the ministerial specialties before you, to assess your own gifts and to begin think about one sort of ministry or another.

4. In addition, I thought it helpful to address a common transitional issue that hits right after seminary is over: "Post Seminary Stress Syndrome."

IDENTITY

5. In "How to Lose Your Ministry" I take a tongue-in-cheek look at the matter of professionalism versus servanthood ministry. This is especially important for the person who has left an environment where success means larger profits, greater numbers, and larger responsibilities (promotions). It is the bane of the ministry, it is hoped that these thoughts will guard you from such temptations.

6. Preaching is at the heart of our identity as mortals called to serve God and man. Thus, I have included a lecture called, "The Justification of Preaching" to counter attacks and contortions of the place of preaching in our ministries.

7. I offer a hymn: "God is Calling Faithful Men."

I trust through each of these lectures or sermons or essays (and hymn), you will open your life up to the Lord of the Harvest and yield yourself to Him. The need of the day is for preachers who will leave all—to follow their call.

WHY YOUNG MEN DON'T GO INTO THE MINISTRY

A CASE OF MISTAKEN IDENTITY

Jesus Christ knew that despite the thrill of following the Creator of the Universe and becoming an Official of His Royal Court—an ambassador of the Kingdom of the Living God—many would not go into the ministry of His Gospel. So, he declared, "The fields are white unto Harvest, but the workers are few. Pray the Lord of the Harvest to send out workers into the fields."

We are seeing a trend today in the ministry. In fact, I think we have a crisis. The average age of seminarians today is thirty-seven years old. Why? Well, I am certain there are a number of sociological reasons for this trend, but I want to offer one that is not always voiced today.

I believe that God still calls young men to go into the ministry at sixteen, seventeen, eighteen and nineteen years if age. It is just that not too many heed God's call.

Because of a few misconceptions, these otherwise outstanding candidates for the ministry opt for business and law and medicine and other similar worthy pursuits.

Then, ten to fifteen years later—if they are not completely burned-out in their career which promised them money, prestige, and influence and brought them only dissatisfaction—they begin to reassess their call to ministry.

Now, there are some (and I was one) who were not called until having already established a first career. The reason? Well, for me it was that my life was so out of order and in complete rebellion at 20 years of age, that the first call I heard was just to surrender to the grace of God in Christ and trust in Him alone for my eternal life! I am thankful that there are many like me in that regard.

But, I am talking today about those faithful disciples who are of younger years and who should be considering God's call to the ministry, but are not because of some misconceptions.

Well, today, is your day. I want to clear up a few of those misconceptions. I believe what we really are facing is a case of mistaken identity.

Why don't young men go into the ministry?

They think money will bring them success and happiness.

The truth? It won't. This is an essential spiritual truth taught in God's Word. Get that settled and then follow me from here. The ministry will not normally make you a wealthy man. The ministry, however, will provide you with everything you need to live materially and it will be fulfilling. What price can be placed on a job that helps people come out of sin into eternal life in Christ? What price can you put on holding the baby of a family you led to Christ and then baptizing that child into the Church? You are there at all of the important times in people's lives, when all others are shut out—you are there—with your pitcher of living water to thirsty souls and your plate of Divine blessings to those who hunger for deeper meaning in life.

They think the Ministry is boring work.

If the ministry is presiding over a dead ceremony once a week, having tea with a well upholstered spinster whose tithes keep your kid in braces, and occasionally braving the elements to lift a hand in the annual church maintenance fund drive—well if that is the ministry—I WANT OUT NOW!

But that is not the ministry. That is a caricature of the job and is far removed from the reality of ministry. The reality is that every week something new is happening. It is true that you preach, you teach, you administer the sacraments, you counsel, you administer, you organize, you lead, but within those unchanging rubrics lie a world of diverse operations and a world of difficult assignments, and a world of decisive opportunities!

In one week, I have saved a marriage, led a family to Christ, met with the leaders of my city, offered hope to a grieving family, taught a class on Evidences for the Resurrection, preached a message on the Doctrine of the Sovereignty of God and dedicated a new building! Where else can you do this?

When I think of the ministry, I think of the words of a great preacher who said, "Do not stoop to be a king when you have been called to preach!"

The ministry is exciting!

They think that Ministers are boring people.

I can understand how some of you feel this way. If the ministry is, as Hollywood often portrays it, milk-toast, weak chinned wimps with old, oversized cardigan sweaters and a liberal message of "have a nice day," then I would think it is boring, as well. If ministers are, as some ministers sinfully portray us, lazy lugs who do little to contribute to the good of anyone except to contribute to the growing size of their pot bellies, then, I would say, "Yes, ministers are boring people."

I would have, you, though, to observe history and conclude for yourself if such is really the case.

Consider the prophets of the Old Testament.

No one reading the life of the Minor prophet Amos could honestly assert that his was a boring life! A simple man called from herding sheep and tending sycamore fruit to preaching to royalty in an apostate kingdom is hardly leading a boring life. Risky? Yes. Influential? Yes. But never boring. The same goes for Moses, Abraham, David, Isaiah, Jeremiah and the rest of those stalwart men of God.

Consider the Apostles.

Whether we consider Peter, who went from being a middle class fisherman to an emboldened preacher to thousands; or Thomas who went from being the skeptic who fell before the risen Christ to the one who, according to tradition, brought the Gospel to India; or the others who gave their lives away for a cause greater than themselves; we are speaking of the very personages who changed the world.

But, I draw your attention to the "least of the Apostles." For the Apostle Paul, following Christ into the ministry meant leaving a career. It meant, for him, facing the very people whom he once persecuted. What a risk. What a change. But, of course, Paul went forward and in doing so became the catalyst in the hands of God that literally changed the course of human history. When historians trace the many and diverse tributaries of world history through Western civilization, the streams begin to merge at the living waters flowing from the consecrated ministry of one changed man: Saul of Tarsus.

Consider the Reformers.

We have mentioned Luther, but what of Calvin? Try doing an INTERNET search for Calvin and you will discover that this one Frenchman has influenced not only religion but politics and economics. Can we truly speak of modern history without mentioning Wycliffe and the translation of the Word of God into English? My dear friends, there is every evidence that ministers of the Gospel have had as much if not more influence on the lives of even the most disinterested modern man or woman as merchants and scientists and artists.

Consider the founders of our nation's institutions.

You cannot speak of the great institutions of higher education without admitting the role of ordained ministers. All of the great Ivy League schools were founded by ministers and many of what became state universities were founded by the clergy. But, if you went further and asked who influenced the great businessmen in our nation, would you probably not begin to list countless ministers of every Christian denomination across the globe?

Consider the leaders of the great social changes in our own country.

Whether you are speaking of the movement to overturn slavery, or to advance civil rights for minorities, or to protect the rights of children and the elderly and the unborn, you will be bound to name the names of famous ministers of the Gospel who led the charge.

Consider the dominant personalities of our day.

Just last night, I watched as Dr. Al Moehler of Southern Baptist Theological Seminary argued for the position of Bible believing Christians in America on Larry King Live. Dr. Moehler is just one of many of today's ministers who are emerging to take the mantle of evangelical leadership from other more famous names like Billy Graham and James Kennedy. Whether you particularly agree with them all or not, you are bound to admit that ministers of the Gospel continue to exert a strong influence on the way we shape our ideas about life and the world around us. and this is my point. You cannot say that the ministry is boring and that business, law, and so forth is a better way to spend your life. Now, it may be a fine pursuit for many, but if you are being called of God to proclaim the unsearchable riches of Christ to a world in need, how can you turn away? If your excuse is that such a career is simply too boring then what will you do with the evidence I have produced to the contrary?

Ministers are not boring people. Some ministers are just bad ministers.

They want to be influential and they think that the ministry is not.

Again, this is a misconception born out of poor ministers and bad Hollywood scripts.

If you want to influence society: be a minister. You can change lives in a local church as a pastor or associate pastor. You can mold lives in a Christian school, college or seminary as a teacher, professor, or as the headmaster. You can travel to unreached people groups and change the course of a whole nation for the rest of history as a missionary. You can change this nation as a church planter.

There is no greater joy than changing one life at a time with the simple news of Jesus Christ—His grace, His atoning sacrifice, His invitation to a new life.

Ministers have been and continue to be the most influential members of society at both the personal level, and in many cases, the national and even world level.

Facing the Truth

The real question is will you face the truth of the ministry as it is or will you hold onto your misconception? To hold on to your misconception is to rule out the ministry as an option before you.

To get real with it, though, is to get risky. It is a risk to give your life up to Jesus Christ and the service of His Kingdom. There is no doubt about it. Ministry is risky. But, pray tell, what great thing has ever been done without it?

I was once frightened of this. I thought that if I gave my life to Christ and to His service, I would be in chains forever.

I read Edmund Clowney's Book, Called to the Ministry, and I came across something very interesting. Martin Luther, the great

Reformer, must have felt the same way as I did. In fact, Luther felt had been given the gifts to become one of the greatest legal minds in all of Europe. Luther was additionally blessed with exceptional gifts in music and might have enjoyed a status on par with the greatest musicians of Germany. But, he was called to the ministry. He said that his call to preach and to teach and to be an ambassador for Jesus Christ had become burdensome to him! Perhaps, Luther, too, was confused as to whether he should pursue these other outstanding fields, but in the end he could not, because he knew he had to give his life to the ministry of the Gospel of Jesus Christ. The ministry had become chains to him. Luther was saying, "In my chains I at last found my freedom."

That is the way I felt. I embraced the chains of the Gospel. Paul's credo became my own: "Woe is me if I preach not the Gospel!"

In those chains, I have found the greatest freedom I have ever known.

Today, I am asking you to consider if God may be calling you to the ministry. I am asking some others of you if God might be calling you to some other form of Christian service.

Jesus said in a parable: "Why have you been standing here all day long doing nothing?" and the unemployed laborers answered, "Because no one has hired us." He said to them, "You also go and work in my vineyard."

How many today will heed the call? How many here will stretch forward your neck and hands and take the yoke of Christ upon you as a minister of the Gospel and find the greatest freedom and fulfillment that young and old men have ever known?

THE MINISTRY OF A SEMINARIAN

FIGHTING THE GOOD FIGHT OF FAITH FROM THE VERY BEGINNING

There are some seminarians who mistakenly believe that once their degree is in hand, they will somehow mystically be transformed into a minister. The reality is that your call should transform you and seminary is, really, your first "duty station" as a minister. Your deportment in your classes and in your relationship to your fellow students, faculty, and administration will forge a pattern for future ministry assignments.

The Seminarian has a ministry. What is it?

A SEMINARIAN'S SCRIPTURE

> But you, man of God, flee from all this, and pursue righteousness, godliness, faith, love, endurance and gentleness. Fight the good fight of the faith. Take hold of the eternal life to which you were called when you made your good confession in the presence of many witnesses. (1 Tim. 6.11-12)

THE MISTAKES OF ROOKIES

As you are going through orientation for training to be pastors, missionaries and various other sorts of Christian workers, there is an orientation of sorts going on another institution in our country—the National Football League.[27] Soon, there will be a great number of rookies (as well as veterans) cut from their teams. In some cases, they are cut because they, rookies and vets alike, succumbed to outside interests rather than concentrating on the things that make for good football players.

So, too, as you are gathered here there are dangers. Some of you can't wait to get going in seminary, but your minds have not grasped

---

[27] This was originally presented as a sermon to new seminarians in the early fall.

the reality that you are now entering the ministry. Some of you imagine that you will go through seminary and then after ordination, some sort of magic dust will be sprinkled on you and you can begin to "act like a minister."

I believe that young Timothy was, in essence, a seminarian under the professor, St. Paul. What Paul says to Timothy in 1 Timothy 6.3–10 is an outline of the way Timothy is to approach his ministry.

I want you to pause this morning and, likewise, consider your ministry as a seminarian, using the charge given us in today's reading.

I. FIRST OF ALL, YOUR MINISTRY IS TO BE A MAN OF GOD (V. 11)

The way Paul addresses Timothy is important. This is a title of honor—of nobility—of character. A man selected for the ministry must be a man of God first and foremost.

1. You will be a Man of God as you make God your first priority.

I would, for instance, advocate serving the Lord on His day and refraining from your studies. Tithe your money and your time to Christ. God needs neither, but you need to prioritize the Lord. Be a man of God.

2. You will be a Man of God as you seek personal holiness.

There is no magic dust at ordination that will make you a Man of God. You must show yourselves approved unto God right now. Use seminary to practice holiness. All eyes are upon you as a model of what a Man of God is to be. Be a man of God.

3. You will be a Man of God as you look upon your studies as sacred.

As a pastor, teacher, missionary or whatever and however you serve, your chief business is always communicating the Word of God and providing God's answers to everyday problems. To do so, you must study. A Man of God is a man who has sat at the feet of Lord and supped with Him from His Word. Use your studies in languages, history, systematic, preaching and liturgics to honor God. Go into every class with the attitude that you are dedicating this to Him. Be a man of God.

Now, look at Paul's explosion of directives to young Timothy. These are God's words to you today.

II. YOUR MINISTRY IS TO TURN YOUR BACK ON THE WORLD (V.11 "...FLEE THESE THINGS...")

Flee what things?

Verses 3–10 tell us about error and greed in the world. Paul mentions pride, useless wrangling of men and philosophical disputes, and discontentment.

You, too, must turn your back on error and greed, which marks the occupations of so many others in the world.

1. Turn your back on Pride.

Pride will attack you in seminary. You may be tempted to be proud because you are in seminary and the rest of your Sunday school class is not. You may become a know-it-all and try to exhibit your newfound theological insights to others. I assure you that others easily discern such pride, and your display will be offensive and hurt your ministry.

I read an anonymous Puritan quote which is helpful to us at this point:

> When God intends to fill a soul He first makes it empty; when He intends to enrich a soul He first makes it poor; when He intends to exalt a soul, He first makes it sensible of its own miseries, wants, and nothingness.

There is nothing so odious as a seminarian filled with pride. It is grievous to those of us who lead you and it hurts the Church in general. Remember that Jesus said the greatest in the Church is the one who serves. Use your theology to help others to drink from the deep wells of the Bible, not as a showy garment that draws attention to yourself.

2. Turn your back on useless wrangling and philosophical disputes.

Now, I don't mean that you should not take up genuine theological issues at seminary. If there is one place where you should be allowed to do so it is here. Iron sharpens iron, the Bible says, and so it must be at seminary.

No, what is prohibited is what the great ancient father, Chrysostom, described as:

> ...poor wretches of sophists shouting and abusing each other, and their disciples, as they call them, squabbling, and many writers of books reading their stupid compositions, and many poets singing their poems, and many jugglers exhibiting their marvels, and many soothsayers giving their meaning of prodigies, and a thousand rhetoricians twisting lawsuits...[28]

The picture is of philosophers putting on a show, craving praise and competing with each other for attention from the crowds.

Now, seminarians can be like that. Ministers can be like that. All show.

It is interesting for me to listen to the questions of many of my fellow elders when a young minister comes up for ordination examination. Often what comes out of their mouths is a display of the last thing they read or some specialized interest they have.

Interesting, too, is to listen to the comments of some seminarians in class. They are eager, like a peacock before a hen, to display their learning for the sake of drawing attention to their intellectual prowess.

It should not be so.

Flee from this and pursue learning with righteousness and an eye towards pleasing God and building up the Church.

---

[28] As quoted in William Barclay, The Daily Bible Study Series: The Letters to Timothy, Titus, and Philemon, Revised Edition, "1 Timothy," (Philadelphia: Westminster Press, 1975), 125.

3. Turn your back on discontentment.

Many of your friends are in graduate school, too, aren't they? —Business Schools, Law Schools, Medical Schools. All of you are on a professional track that will lead to an important place in society. But, you, seminarian, are in a different class: poor! The others are generally well financed with the potential for huge profits in the future.

Going to seminary, working two jobs, your wife and kids also chipping in to make ends meet—and trying to juggle a schedule to do it all and with no promise of a huge monetary windfall in the future—can lead to discontentment.

Just remember this: While others are learning about profit margins, court cases, and anatomical Latin, you, my friend, are pursuing God and the ministry of Jesus Christ. With all due respect and gratitude for the other professions, in the end, your work will greatly outlast any fruit they will have gathered in this life. You will baptize converts, catechize children, marry couples, console the grieving and, week after week, proclaim the unsearchable riches of Jesus Christ that is able to save souls and change our world!

Whenever you get discontent with the life of a seminarian, only consider the high and holy calling to which you aspire and the eternal life that you are gathering for yourself and those who are touched by your ministry.

CONCLUSION

In conclusion, your ministry is (1) to be a Man of God and to (2) turn Your Back on the World.

How do you do that?

Paul gives the answer:

> ...Pursue righteousness, godliness, faith, love, patience, gentleness, Fight the good fight of faith, lay hold on eternal life, to which you were also called... (1 Timothy 6.11,12)

In other words, be actively engaged with becoming more like Christ.

I will never forget when I sat where you are now sitting. I had worked and planned and dreamed of seminary for a long time. Finally, at last, I found myself sitting in the Orientation Chapel. My mind was spinning with thoughts of studying theology under my well grounded and all wise professors. I was a bit "heady" about it all and just a little proud of being there.

Then, Dr. Robert Reymond, who was our Professor of Systematic Theology at Knox Theological Seminary, addressed us in that chapel. He ended his message with words that reached out and grabbed my heart and stirred me to the depths of my sin-recovering soul:

> Brothers, if you go through three to four years of seminary, attending all of the classes, reading all of the required texts, listening to all of the lectures, memorizing all of the charts and paradigms, passing all of the examinations, and are handed that sheepskin...and yet don't love Jesus more and know Him better at the end than at the beginning, then you have failed, and your time here will have been a waste.

You now have a ministry. You are a seminarian. Flee from the world of error and greed and take upon yourself, even now, the mantle of humility and servanthood which marks every great minister of the Gospel...and lay hold of the mind and character and perfect will of Almighty God who called you to the ministry. Amen.

WHAT COLOR IS YOUR PULPIT?

DISCOVERING YOUR PLACE IN THE MINISTRY

We are assuming that God has called you to the ministry, that you, in fact, are possessed of both the inward and outward calls to the ordained Gospel ministry. You are either on your way to seminary, just graduating seminary, just leaving seminary, or, perhaps, are reading this as you are well into your vocation. Assuming that, I want to discuss a topic that leads not a few ordained ministers to a place of near despair: "now what?"

"What Color is Your Parachute" is the title of a popular guide to helping individuals match their gifts and dreams to the suitable career.[29] This chapter is, similarly, concerned about discussing and, hopefully assisting you in the process of helping you match your gifts and dreams to the suitable need within the ministry. The vision of this chapter, indeed, this book, is to strengthen you and in some way stir you on to a good "landing" in the ordained ministry.

The ministry is not, of course, about self-actualization and self-fulfillment (the apparent overarching interest of many "career help" books). Jesus came to serve and we are no better than our Master. Rather, the ministry is God's answer to the spiritual needs of the world. Men and women are saved, sanctified, taught, fed and clothed, put in their right minds, so to speak, and called to a better way through the instrumentality of the ordained ministry. "What Color is Your Pulpit" then, should be a question to those who are intent on giving their lives away to God and to others. This is decidedly not an appeal to only your self-fulfillment, but to help you consider God's best place for you within the ministry.

Now, I entitle this, "What Color is Your Pulpit" and I don't mean that every ministry involves a pulpit ministry in a local church. I do, though, mean to say that every area of ministry, every grouping and subset of the ordained task is and must be in some way living out the

---

[29] Richard Nelson Bolles, What Color Is Your Parachute?: 2000 Edition: A Practical Manual for Job-Hunters & Career-Changers, 30th Rev edition (Berkeley, California: Ten Speed Press, 1999).

Ministry of the Word. When I say "pulpit" I am referring here to the task of preaching and administering the Sacraments or Ordinances of the Church of Jesus Christ. I am saying that we are all, if we are Ministers of the Gospel, at our most basic job description: just preachers.

I am the Chairman of the Candidates and Credentials Committee of a regional judicatory in my own denomination (The Presbyterian Church in America). One of my jobs, along with my fellow presbyters, is to examine ministers and their calls to see whether the work to which they are being called is meet with the goals of ordination. There was once a man that came to us who described the work to which he was called. This fellow, who had been working at this position for some time, described his leadership of this particular foreign mission. It all sounded very good and was a profitable and worthy ministry. The question that our committee had, though, was whether or not he needed to be ordained in order to do the ministry. Ministers are called to be God's agents of Word and Sacrament. There are many ways that Word and Sacrament works its way out in various agencies of the Church and of respective missions (and we will consider some of them here). There are also outstanding ministries and positions within those ministries that do not require Word and Sacrament to reach their stated goals. Several of us determined that in this fellow's case, he did not need ordination credentials to carry out the functions of that job.

Every ministry must have a pulpit. Every ministry in the Church, which requires an ordained Minister of the Gospel to fill it, has a place for Word and Sacrament, in some tangible fashion.

The look and feel of the pulpit changes as one observes the various roles in the Church. The Senior Pastor of a multi-staff church is different from the solo pastorate in some ways. The Assistant Minister for Youth has different goals and requires distinctly different gifts and even personalities than a church planter for Eastern Europe. The itinerant evangelist, the Seminary professor, the college campus chaplain, the military chaplain are all different (and all alike, in that they are all ministries of Word and Sacrament).

Where do you fit in?

HOW DO YOU KNOW?

If I didn't believe that God would show you where, in fact, He wants you, I would do better to not write this chapter or this book. But, I do, indeed, believe that the Lord Himself will show you His will for you. Did Christ not tell us to "Ask, and it will be given to you; seek and you will find; knock, and it will be opened to you?"[30]

Begin, then, with earnest prayer in this regard. He called you. He will be faithful to guide you. As He led you to surrender to His call to preach the Gospel, He will likewise make Himself known to you in this area.

In this matter of "which ministry is the best one for me" I would like to offer a few simple indicators, or "signposts" that will guide you in your journey. I believe that Romans 12.3–8 provides a fine paradigm for considering which ministry is for you. In that passage, St. Paul, after calling the Romans to transformed living in this world, reminds them that, they will live this out in different ways.

> For as we have many members in one body, but all the members do not have the same function...having then gifts differing according to the grace that is given to us... (vv. 4 and 6).

The first signpost along the way is most assuredly in your heart right now, or is being formed within you. What is it? Passion. Paul talks about a different grace given to each of us by God. Grace is the operative key to our salvation and our ministry, as well. Grace is given us at the point of our need, and when we receive that grace at that need we are healed—we are saved.

God will give you a passion for something, for someone, for some need, arising out of that grace in your own life. This is the first great indicator. Show me a recovered alcoholic that God has called to preach, and I will show you a great candidate to minister to alcoholics. Of course, there are many fine ministers in that capacity who never had to fight that battle. I would submit, though, that when God touches your life in one particular area, He gives you a passion for others who are still in the sin and misery from which you were delivered. So, I would say, just go to the Lord and see what He has done in your life and go from there.

---

[30] Matthew 7.7 (NKJV)

So, "passion" is the first signpost, and I would submit that "giftedness" is the second. The Apostle Paul mentions prophecy, service, teaching, exhorting, giving, leading, and mercy. I don't believe that this is intended as the exhaustive list of New Testament gifts but is an example of the variety of God-given gifts. Now, if you have a passion and a gift that are compatible—and there is a need and an outward calling—then there is probably a divine match. Of course, if your passion is seeing youth discipled, but you and others assess you as lacking fundamental qualities that endear you to teenagers, you obviously don't have a match. Therefore, passion and giftedness must be linked.

Perhaps a word should be said, as well, about measuring instruments. There are a variety of psychological tests, personality inventories, and personal gift inventories that are available to help you in this. I am not in the least opposed to these as a matter of principle. I think the Myers-Briggs® and the DISC® temperament profiles are quite helpful. But, when I have taken these tests (and I have taken them before, during and after seminary training), I have found that they usually change little and tell me what I generally already know (not that affirmation is not needed—it is, and I commend these instruments to you).

I urge anyone wanting to know "what color is my pulpit" to begin with a recollection of the grace of God in your life, the passion and faith which God gave you, and your gifts and interests which you and others see in you.

THE VARIETIES OF MINISTRIES CONSIDERED

In an effort to help you, I want to address several traditional ministry positions and provide what I think are the passions, gifts and interests peculiar to each one. Unless otherwise noted, each position is assumed to be a "home" ministry—that is, not a foreign missionary experience.

SOLO PASTOR

The solo pastor is what most people think about when they think about the ministry. Of course, there is variety within this particular ministry (and all of the other jobs I will list). There are solo pastors in rural churches, new churches, churches in need of revitalization, and urban churches. Each of these respective positions demands a peculiar mix of passions and gifts. I want to concentrate on the "common denominator" issues of the solo pastor, no matter where that may exist.

I once read an essay in which the writer reminisced about his childhood pastor. He wrote that everything he knew about theology and church and servanthood had its origin in that Godly man who dressed in khakis every day except Sunday, who could be seen during the week sometimes walking through the small community hospital, sometimes cutting the grass at church, and sometimes knocking down dirt dauber nests out of the corner of the sanctuary with a broom handle, and always ready to tell you about Jesus Christ.

That is not a bad thumbnail sketch of the solo pastor.

Passions: The solo pastor is usually a minister who likes serving in smaller churches, less administration, less leadership of staff, and more hands-on ministry. Indeed, the solo pastor has a passion for equipping the saints for the work of ministry in a real one-on-one fashion. The person cut out for this position should be one who, perhaps, finds as much or more satisfaction by leading a workday at the church as by leading an evangelistic campaign for a major city. To the solo pastor, there is no greater joy than in shepherding the flock through one-on-one visitation at their homes, in their places of employment, or at the graduation ceremony.

Warnings: High-energy drivers who see ministry in larger portions may find the solo pastorate confining. Yet, it may be you need to discover the joy and contentment of a solo pastorate, even if you prefer a multi-staff church, or a church plant or a mission agency. Alternatively, if you see your calling as primarily a shepherd, not one who delegates the caring to other shepherds, then, this is a place for you.

MULTI-STAFF SENIOR PASTOR

The Senior Pastor of a church is essentially the minister responsible for the equipping and shepherding work of the congregation, who, because of the size of the congregation or the level of competency and/or efficiency expected by church leadership, leads a staff of ordained and non-ordained people to carry out the pastoral charge. The Senior Pastor, thus, delegates respective components of the ministerial task to people with matching competencies (Youth Pastor, Visitation Pastor, Christian Education Pastor, etc.).

Passions: This ministerial profile calls for an individual who is generally a leader (leaders like to lead and usually seek out positions that are not in more or less isolation, such as a solo pastorate), and who sees things in terms of "the big picture." The Senior Pastor position may be seen as an "executive" position, but in truth, those who lead like that are prone to get into trouble in one way or another. The Senior Pastor is the senior servant. His job is still to equip the saints for the work of ministry—it is just that it is accomplished with more than one person.

Warnings: Some are prone to idealize this position. Some see the job as "higher up the ladder" than say - a solo pastor. The best Senior Pastors will quickly tell you that there is nothing glamorous about bearing the burden of either a large congregation or a congregation with high expectations. Moreover, the Senior Pastor's roles as fellow minister and yet supervisor to other ministers is a tricky one that has few counterparts in the business world. In order to succeed, the Senior Pastor spends or should spend a great deal of time in prayer, in encouraging and praying with and for his staff, and in preparing to lead from the "big group" (i.e., The Worship Services, Boards) of the church, rather than the smaller groups (i.e., Sunday School, Bible studies).

MULTI-STAFF ASSOCIATE PASTOR

Following on the back of Senior Pastor is our consideration of his specialty ministers. The Minister of Youth, of Christian education, of visitation, and so forth, fulfill the overall pastoral charge in such a church.

Passions: One primary passion must be for the specialty itself, whatever that might be. You see yourself as working in a team environment, encouraging others and looking to other peers for your encouragement. You are more comfortable in smaller group settings, in fulfilling the mandates rather than setting them. Of primary importance, in my opinion, is the personal trait of what the Bible calls, "helps." You are a supporter rather than the "up front" leader.

Warnings: This is not a place to hide out. Some try to hide out in the specialties because they are not fond of any sort of leadership.

All ministers are leaders of God's people. The staff minister is responsible for leading in his particular department. Similarly, some might think this is a good place to hide from the "harder" work of either a solo pastor or senior pastor. Again, this is patently wrong. I have known staff ministers to actually spend more time working at their position than senior pastors. The highly specialized nature of the ministry seems to encourage people to think that you have nothing else to do but serve them. As a result, departmental ministry can often bear the burden of doing your primary ministry task, plus filling in for the Senior Pastor when he is out, and, in mega churches, covering other departments during vacation season or when there is a vacancy. This, like all ministries, is hard work—or should be. There is much work in the harvest fields of our Lord. Ministers are called to realize this and embrace it, not hide from it or whine about it.

CHURCH PLANTER

All ministries that you see up and running were once just a man and a vision. Once that church you attend, that seminary you are going to, or that hospital you are recovering in was the heartbeat of that entrepreneurial spirit who saw God's kingdom and human need and said to himself, "This cannot be. God is too great and the condition here too bad. Who will go and build? Who has seen God's plan and will dare stand in the gap of this age and announce that plan? I must."

This is the soul of the church planter. Now, when I say "church planter" I would include all of those more "apostolic" souls who work outside of the settled ministries of the church. They may be planting churches or schools, or nursing homes, or television and radio ministries, but the common denominator is their resolve to change the way things are by creating a new extension of God's kingdom for the need. Often church planters end up as solo pastors, senior pastors, para church ministry leaders, and even itinerant evangelists.

Passions: A great deal has been written about church planters in our day. The study of the assessment and sending of church planters has become quite scientific. I would recommend that those of you interested in further exploration of that ministry take advantage of the several good publications out on the subject. For my purposes here, let me just say that the ministry of a church planter always begins with one who feels things deeply. The church planter looks across a community and sees a need and feels that need himself. He goes to God and believes that God is telling him to go and meet the need. He hears the cry of the oppressed—be they suburbanites drowning in a meaningless neighborhood of materialism or inner city families being torn apart at the heart by drugs, gang violence and hopelessness. When the church planter senses the will of God in these matters, it leads him to do something. By nature, then, the church planter is a risk taker. The church planter does not ask, "What will be the salary?" The church planter is consumed by the vision of the ministry, itself, and will build the infrastructure to support any salary or no salary. Like St. Paul (the model for all such ministers), the church planter will "mend tents" to fulfill his calling. Another necessary trait of all such ministers is the God-given gift to articulate their vision in such a way that others begin to see the vision and gather around it. Churches are planted, not because Mr. and Mrs. Jones liked the nursery facilities and so joined Pastor Steve's church since there is no nursery and there are no facilities. Mr. and Mrs. Jones joined the church because when Pastor Steve casts his vision of God and His kingdom, Mr. and Mrs. Jones, maybe for the first time in their lives, could see what was not there and believe, somehow, that it would happen. This is the gift of the church planter—the gift, really, of faith.

Warnings: The one who see himself as a church planter can, without the controlling insight and wisdom, also see himself as a nonconformist, a real maverick, or often, through the process of casting vision and leading the charge for following the vision, become a maverick. God did not call us to be lone wolves, or loose cannons. Paul's ministry, though given to him by Christ personally, started officially when Barnabas brought the new preacher to the Church officials (Acts 9.27).[31] Even the great "church planter" of Tarsus recognized the divine limitations and parameters placed over individual ministers. When a conflict arose in the early church over the issue of grace, Paul appealed to the larger Church at Jerusalem to settle the matter. The Lord has not made lone wolves, but relational creatures and has put us in a pack; it's called the Church. We also don't just fire at random, but aim our cannons in harmony with each other. We are the army of the Lord, not guerilla

---

[31] "But Barnabas took him and brought him to the apostles. And he declared to them how he had seen the Lord on the road, and that He had spoken to him, and how he had preached boldly at Damascus in the name of Jesus. (Acts 9.27, NKJV)."

mercenaries. Submission and servanthood are watchwords for all of us. The church planter must recognize that the very same passion and giftedness which propels him onto the field to meet the need, and to gather others around who will see his vision, can get him into trouble. I have known several church planters who forfeited their ministries because of a failure to either see this trait or to guard against it. Conversely, some might see this ministry as attractive without coming to terms with the tremendous physical and emotional energy that is expended. Moreover, this ministry, perhaps more than any other ministry type, requires a 110% commitment from the entire family. Church planting is an all-consuming ministry that has its weekly ups and downs. Let no one enter this ministry who is not assessed, called, trained, prepared, and prayed up for the work. Many have tried it and can testify to its rigors. Yet, for the one who is called, it becomes one of the most gratifying things a minister can do.

FOREIGN MISSIONARY

Passions: Whether one serves as an evangelist, church planter, administrator, teacher, or pastor, the one thing that all foreign missionaries must possess is what I call a passion for, as well as the accompanying personal resources for, cross cultural ministry. This is an interest, ability to and even desire to relate to others in another culture. It involves an interest in language, cultures, and a great sense of mission. I have found that many foreign missionaries recognized this gift before they were ever called to a foreign mission field. Indeed the presence of the passion, itself, in some way led to their awareness and acceptance of the call. There are other gifts necessary for a foreign missionary, but this gift of cross-cultural adaptability is the most obvious.

Warnings: One might approach foreign missions like a high-school boy dreaming over a Navy recruiting poster: "Join the Navy and see the world." Don't do it. Foreign missions requires like all types of ministry a deep sense of call, devout commitment to Christ—and because at times the fruit of the ministry is not borne or witnessed for many years—a strong kingdom vision.

INSTITUTIONAL CHAPLAIN

Passions: A chaplain in a hospital or a prison does not only prepare sermons and conduct services and do visitation like other ministers, the chaplain does so within the context of a given institution. The institution may be a hospital or battlefield or prison but, wherever it is, that institution informs and controls the ministry setting. In short, I believe one has to normally have a strong sense of connection to the ministry environment and the people there as well as for the ministry. Thus, as I heard one old chaplain put it,

> "I'm not very smart. So when I was deciding what I would do with my life, I knew that a few things would help me decide. Number one, I loved God. Number two I loved soldiers because I was one. Number three, I could preach. I put those things into my little computer and out came an Army chaplain. and I've been doing that ever since."

It's hard to imagine anyone putting it any better than that.

Warnings: If you don't love the institution, or the people there, this is not the place for you. Go minister in a church or as an evangelist. You will find institutional ministry confining and restrictive unless you have the passion for the institution and the ministry challenges it presents.

PARA CHURCH MINISTER/ADMINISTRATOR

Some ministers are leaders of Christian organizations who work along side of churches to get the Gospel out, to disciple new believers, and to facilitate Gospel ministry in any of a number of ways. There are, of course, many specialties needed in para church ministries. For our concern, I am interested in introducing the work of a minister who labors in administration.

Passion: This person loves the big idea of ministry and recognizes that his contribution is important to seeing it continue. He is chosen of God to lead, to supervise, to conduct and carry out the work of the ministry. As with all ordained tasks, in my opinion, this requires a preacher. But, while the administrator may preach and teach in pulpits and classrooms, he is equally at home in casting the vision for the team, the ministry and leading others to achieve it.

Warnings: Administrators and leaders of Christian organizations do not necessarily get the same preaching and teaching opportunities as their parish counterparts. Furthermore, there is normally no regular administration of the sacraments in this position. There is no liturgical leadership involved with leading a parachurch organization. You need to recognize this fact and reconcile it with your own sense of giftedness and calling.

TEACHER/PROFESSOR

Ministers of the Gospel have always been at the forefront of instruction and guidance. Teaching, of course, is the very essence of what it is to be an ordained minister. The minister who is a teacher in a secondary school or a professor in a college, university, or seminary brings not only his academic discipline to bear on the students, but does so with the heart of the preacher.

Passions: Obviously, you must love teaching and students and the thrill of the classroom. Working with other teachers and with the overall goals of the school also plays a crucial part in being happy as a minister-teacher. Moreover, I have found that the one who fits this description also has adapted well to the academic community with its many idiosyncrasies. Because most professors will have done academic work beyond the Master of Divinity degree (i.e., Master of Theology, Doctor of Philosophy, Doctor of Theology), one gets a good opportunity to test the fit.

Warnings: A teacher in a classroom or a professor in a department are not the same, again, as a pastor in a church. Nor does he only teach. A professor invariably will have to write, research, and work with administration on various projects ranging from recruitment of students to the raising of funds for the school. If you consider that a waste of time when you could be giving the Gospel to teenagers in a retreat setting, for example, obviously, you need to think about a different color of pulpit.

POST SEMINARY STRESS SYNDROME

THE CRISIS OF LEAVING THE ACADEMY AND HITTING THE FIELD

Hopefully seminary will be a blessed time of preparation. Much of that time and a significant degree of the prospective blessing will have been the friendships, the collegiality, and the joy of fellowship with other seminarians and their families.

Once you walk the aisle, accept the call or appointment, and settle in to your ministry, though, there may—or should I say most probably will—come a time of testing. I call that time of testing "the Post Seminary Stress Syndrome." It's not exactly like the "post war syndrome" where young men struggle with the pressing realities of civilian life even as they reflect upon, have nightmares of, and seek to work out the horrors of the battlefield. But, there are some similarities. There will come some times of reflecting, synthesizing, and sorting out.

I am an Army Reserve chaplain. I was attending a clinic on suicide prevention at The Menninger Clinic as a part of my chaplaincy training. It had been several years since I had left the seminary for my first assignment: church planting. I had been pastoring the church I had planted, and was at that time contemplating another call that had come before me. The speaker that day, Dr. W. Walter Menninger, was presenting a paper entitled, "Adaptation and Morale: Predictable Responses to Life Change."[32] Dr. Menningers' presentation that day dealt with the matter of coping with change. Indeed, the research sought to examine the stages of transition in the life of a Peace Corp volunteer from acceptance to "arrival" and on through "engagement" "acceptance" and "reentry" - or reassignment to another place of service. I listened intently because as the physician talked, I had one of those common yet amazing human moments where I felt that he was talking directly to me.

---

[32] Menninger, W.W. (1988). Adaptation and Morale: Predictable Responses to Life Change. Topeka, Kansas. Bulletin of the Menninger Clinic, Vol. 52, No.3, May, pages 198-210.

Indeed, the study, which chronicled the morale of individuals, put forth a proposition that the measurement is true of other life changes. I, for one, can validate their study!

THE STAGES OF THE POST SEMINARY EXPERIENCE

The Menninger Clinic study revealed that what the Peace Corp volunteers had experienced and displayed could be predicted for others in similar life change situations. Dr. Menninger identified the predictable responses of individuals going through the stages of change as the "morale curve." He went on to say that the "morale curve" is universal.

As I listened and thought about it, I concluded that what happened to me was exactly what the Menninger clinic reported had happened to the Peace Corp folks in their study. From talking to other ministers and watching quite a few seminarians, I would say that it happens to all of us in one way or another.

The study was given in order to help chaplains assess potentials for suicide. I trust no one reading this will even consider that transition from the seminary to the field leads one to consider suicide. Yet, the feelings, which Dr. Menninger describes in his study, are quite descriptive of what you might go through.

Of primary concern in all of this is "adaptability." If you understand the feelings you are experiencing and can recognize that in some way it is even "normal" to feel these things, perhaps, you can adapt and grow through them. Menninger, in his paper, referred to S.C. Kobasa's 1979 study, in which the author wrote:

> ...those who have a greater sense of control over what occurs in their lives will remain healthier than those who feel powerless in the face of external forces. Part of that control is cognitive control, 'the ability to interpret, appraise, and incorporate various sorts of stressful events into an ongoing life plan, and, thereby, deactivate their jarring effects.'[33]

---

[33] Ibid., page 209. Dr. Menninger is quoting from Kobasa, S.C. (1979). "Stressful life events, personality, and health: An inquiry into hardiness." Journal of Personality and Social Psychology, 37, 1-11.

With thanksgiving for Dr. Menninger's work, then, I offer his findings and seek to apply them to our situation: The transition from seminarian to minister. I do so with the prayer that many will be informed, prepared, and thus spared the "jarring effects" of that time.

STAGE ONE: THE CRISIS OF ARRIVAL

Menninger wrote that during this stage,

> ...because the individual had entered this situation with deliberation and conscious intent and had survived a selection process, the mood or morale was high. But along with enthusiasm and excitement and sometimes unrealistic euphoria, the volunteers manifested some degree of apprehension and concern about their ability to meet the challenge.[34]

I had left seminary like a fireball. I had enjoyed a tremendous time of preparation at my own seminary. I had relished the opportunity to immerse myself in study for three years. I had been blessed by mentor relationships with several of my professors. I enjoyed the camaraderie of my fellow seminarians. Having gone to seminary full time, worked full time, and interned part time, I had been living on a very fast-paced schedule for a very long time. My vision of the ministry was big. My expectations of the ministry and for certain immediate results from my ministry were unrealistically high.

As I hit the field—in my case it was to plant a new church—I maintained a strong vision of what I was called to do, but I suddenly, even abruptly, encountered what Kalervo Oberg called "culture shock."[35] This was really shocking to me, because I was from the area! The culture shock had nothing to do with Overland Park, Kansas: it had to do with the abrupt loss of my seminary environs, and the loss of peers and mentors to help me interpret my mission and my mission field. I even felt that the loss of my fast paced schedule—work, school, internship, family all rolled into one—was destabilizing.

---

[34] Ibid., page 200.

[35] Ibid., page 206.

I was experiencing "the anxiety that results from losing all one's familiar cues. These cues include the thousand and one ways in which we orient ourselves to the situations of daily life..."[36]

I went forward. I did the work. But, I carried a load of loneliness at times that brought despair. In fact, I looked at what was happening to me—a new church being planted, a beautiful home, a new child in our home, a lovely community—and wondered why I should be so down. Sociologist Peter Marris (1975) wrote about this problem:

> Since our ability to cope with life depends on making sense of what happens to us, anything which threatens to invalidate our conceptual structures of interpretation is profoundly disruptive... The impulses of conservatism—to ignore or avoid events which do not match our understanding, to control deviation from expected behavior, to isolate innovation and sustain the segregation of different aspects of life—are all means to defend our ability to make sense of life.[37]

I wished I had known then what I know now: There is a powerful emotional impact that comes as one moves through the crisis of arrival. It will not last forever, but it might get worse before it gets better.

STAGE TWO: THE CRISIS OF ENGAGMENT

How long did all of that take? It depends, of course, but it may have been only four months from arrival to engagement.[38]

The crisis now intensifies and the uneasiness of Stage One turns rotten in Stage Two.

---

[36] Ibid., page 207. This is a quote from Foster, G.M. (1962). *Traditional cultures: and the impact of technological change.* New York: Harper & Row.

[37] Ibid., page 206. See Marris, Peter. *Loss and change.* Garden City, NY: Anchor Press/Doubleday. 1975.

[38] According to Menninger's Table, "Comparison of Stages of Adjustment to New Life Situations." See Table 1 in his paper, page 205.

IDENTITY

> The crisis of engagement reflects the realization of the extent of losses—both real and imagined—in the new situation.[39]

> The crisis of engagement involves coming to grips with a changed pattern of relationships.[40]

You have lost seminary. You may be in the greatest ministry in the world, but a significant shift has occurred in your life. You had expectations and they are not exactly as planned. "Is this the ministry?" you say to yourself.

You may begin to show symptoms of depression. You spend too much time at Starbucks and not enough time in the study. You have stopped working out. You no longer set the clock at night. You say, "I'll wake up when I wake up."

This is a critical time for the minister. All of his training and commitment and sacrifice may be lost in a single decision.

What happens next?

You quit. Or, you go on.

Elizabeth Kubler-Ross, the Roman Catholic nun whose work, On Death and Dying provided insight into the grieving process, called this stage by another name: Bargaining.

You have left seminary. Those days are behind you. Maybe your vision was great, but your expectation of how that vision would work its way out practically was a little off.

You are at a crossroads. Remember your Lord's words:

> I will never leave you nor forsake you.

I was winging my way across the Atlantic Ocean for Ph.D. Research at Cardiff, Wales when, in the midst of this crisis, I read these words from a book I had Providentially brought with me:

---

[39] Ibid., page 208.

[40] Ibid.

> Whatever stage of a pastor's life you're in, bloom where you're planted. Don't regret it. Don't find fault with it. Don't be obsessed with going to another stage. See what God will do for you where you are. Let Him use your gifts and abilities to His glory, and I'll guarantee you, one day, some time, some place—just as surely as you're reading these words—you'll look back on this passage in your ministry and say, 'Thank you, God. Thank You for giving me the courage. Thank You for giving me the patience. Thank You that I didn't quit.'[41]

I commend that to anyone reading these words today. Don't stop. Go on and run the race that is before you.

STAGE THREE: THE CRISIS OF ACCEPTANCE

Menninger wrote:

> The crisis of acceptance reflects the achievement of a new sense of self, with a restructuring of emotional forces and relationships. For most people, this restructuring represents a new equilibrium, with greater freedom...

Eleven to fifteen months have passed. You're through the storm. You are home free. It could be that you saw your crisis for what it is—and I want to discuss that in a few lines from now. It could be that you turned down the other call, decided not to return to business or industry. You decided not to surround yourself with people whom you were sure would tell you what you wanted to hear. Instead, you braced yourself for truth and the wounds of a true friend.[42]

Now is when your training and your relationships and the nurturing years of seminary life really pay dividends. You might also say that this is the point when your theology takes on legs. You now synthesize reality and theory.

---

[41] Loudon, Jr., H.B., Editor, Refresh, Renew, Revive (Colorado Springs, CO: Focus on the Family Publishing) 1996, 196.

[42] "Faithful are the wounds of a friend, But the kisses of an enemy are deceitful." (Proverbs 27.6 NKJV)

The real beneficiaries of this move are your parishioners—whoever they are. For now, your sermons will take on a fresh delivery. Your illustrations will be more colorful, your applications wiser. Menninger says that this time is marked by "activism." You are productive again, maybe for the first time since seminary.

Look close and you'll find that you're also happy again.

STAGE FOUR: THE CRISIS OF REENTRY

This stage only happens if there is a conclusion to your ministry. For many of us there will be. It may be precipitated by any number of events, but you recognize the Spirit who called you into the ministry, urging you to follow Him through a new door.

But, this time you will note that there is a great difference in the way you are processing the call. In Stage Two, you were ready to run. You were discontent. You were anxious. You were moving towards depression.

Now, if in fact one ministry is ending and another beginning, you are walking with the Lord. You are exploring God's calling with a healthy head and heart.

Just remember. Every change will signal the possible—yea, probable—trigger that will launch you again into another cycle of stages. Remember? This is supposed to be predictable.

But, now you know.

I believe that the result of education is the accumulation of metaphors and constructs and paradigms. The person who has the most metaphors in the quiver is the most educated. The person who knows which metaphor—which construct or paradigm—to draw from the quiver at the appropriate time is a wise man.

May you go forward in your ministry richly endowed with such wisdom.

"CRISIS" AS A WORK OF THE SPIRIT

I wrote earlier of the prized place in which we see things for what they are.

Perhaps what happens to us is not as clinical as it might seem. Perhaps it not simply a study of empirical data and predictable behavioral science. Perhaps it is the continuing work of the Spirit.

The ministry of Jesus began with a baptism. Not just a baptism but, according to the Scriptures, his inauguration into the public ministry for which He was sent to earth was a supernatural event that was accompanied by the Holy Spirit coming down like a dove, a voice from heaven. His calling, His ministry, His mission, was affirmed.

But, then, the Scriptural record takes a sharp turn from the baptism to the wilderness.

> Then Jesus was led up by the Spirit into the wilderness to be tempted by the devil. (Matthew 4.1, NKJV)

Mark puts it another way:

> Immediately the Spirit drove Him into the wilderness. (Mark 1.12, NKJV)

This is an amazing passage to consider. The Third Person of the Trinity drives the Second Person of the Trinity into a wilderness to be tempted by the Evil One.

There we know that Satan came against the Son of God in those forty days. We may read quickly through the narrative without sensing the aching hunger, imagining the parched mouth, the sun-stroked brow, and the easy way out that was always a possibility before the Creator-in-flesh.

> If You are the Son of God, throw Yourself down.[43]

But Christ answered each temptation with the Word of God. Every "fiery dart" was quenched.

I am saying to you that we are no better than our Master. If He, O wonder of wonders, went from the voice of the Father and the anointing of the Spirit in public baptism to the voice of Satan and the "abandonment" of the Spirit in an isolated wilderness cell, shall we hope to do better?

---

[43] Matthew. 4.6

Could it be that your Post Seminary Stress Syndrome is really a gracious act of the Lord, preparing you, humbling you, refining you, and, yes, even blessing you?

Remember that the story ends with angels coming to minister to the Lord in the wilderness.

I testify to you, dear reader, that I have enjoyed that sweet consolation. I have passed through the wilderness of the early ministry years. But, what I once cursed in my spirit, I now embrace as a gift. For had I never endured the dreaded stages of the Syndrome, those heart-wrenching days of hunger, thirst, and temptation to take the easy way out, I would have never experienced the succor of angels.

HOW TO LOSE YOUR MINISTRY WHILE EXCELLING IN YOUR PROFESSION

A TONGUE-IN-CHEEK CALL TO SERVANTHOOD IN THE MINISTRY

I challenge everyone considering the ministry or for that matter every one who is engaged in the work of the pastorate to mark this verse and consider it well:

> Therefore I endure everything for the sake of the elect, that they too may obtain the salvation that is in Christ Jesus, with eternal glory. (2 Timothy 2.10, NIV)

"KEEPING UP APPEARANCES" Or PROFESSIONALISM WITHOUT HEART

My wife and I love the BBC comedy hit, "Keeping Up Appearances." It's the story of an upper middle income woman named Hyacinth Bucket (which she pronounces "Bouquet") who struggles to maintain the façade of high society in the presence of lesser mortals. At exactly the right moment in each show when she is trying to impress her neighbors with her good taste, along comes her very low society relatives to blow her cover!

The Methodist clergyman and writer Charles Merrill Smith wrote a tongue-in-cheek book for preachers a few decades ago entitled, "How to Become Bishop Without Being Religious."[44] It was a poignant satire about keeping up appearances while sacrificing your ministry. Smith essentially shows that, like Hyacinth, keeping up appearances in the ministry is a sham.

I want to borrow his approach to express the truth of God's Word to a potentially devastating and most often silent killer in the ministry: professionalism without a heart.

---

[44] Charles Merrill Smith, *How to Become a Bishop Without Being Religious* (Garden City, New York: Doubleday and Company, 1965).

I do not mean to say that we are not to be professional. I do not mean to charge that those of us who seek to improve our ministries through education and associating with others in the ministry are necessarily wrong to do so. For certainly, if we are improving, then it stands to naturally reason that we will serve our people better.

What I mean when I say "professionalism without heart" is that condition of ministers (and I believe that we are all subject throughout our lives to this insufferable propensity) which prioritizes utility over passion.

To put it another way, professionalism without heart means to do ministry without getting dirty.

Paul must have known that Timothy faced this possibility. In our passage, the Apostle encourages the younger minister to be extravagant with his service to the saints at Ephesus. He calls for a "hands-in-the earth" approach to ministry.

We need to hear this today. You and I both know that we can lose our ministries and still excel in our professions as ministers and church leaders.

In keeping with the spirit of Smith's sarcastic title, I want to show you from God's Word how to lose your ministry and actually excel in your profession.

Follow me closely...

I. YOU CAN LOSE YOUR MINISTRY AND EXCEL IN YOUR PROFESSION IF YOU DO IT THE EASY WAY. (V 3)

Now, St. Paul says in verse three that we are to

> Endure hardship with us like a good soldier of Christ Jesus. (2 Timothy 2.3, NIV)

Paul uses the metaphor of a soldier in warfare. When Paul writes, "endure hardship" I know what he is meaning.

I remember in my officer basic training as an Army Reserve chaplain. We had to crawl under live fire on a beach about 100 yards long. I remember the horror of the sound of incoming missiles. It was a struggle to crawl beneath fences and around exploding bunkers. I remember saying that if I got to the end of that beach without getting hurt, I would never want to "soldier" again! Of course, as soon as I got my breath again, we had to head out in a night patrol through a dense forest and endure the tension of possible booby traps and the ever-present hazard of enemies hiding in the brush coming out to attack us. Now, it was all training and not real. But, I can tell you that I slept well that night. Soldiering is hard work!

Each of us called to preach the Gospel of Christ and to labor in governing the spiritual affairs of the Church of Jesus Christ have the responsibility to fight the good fight of faith as soldiers. It's like crawling across a beach with live fire when you are seeking to lead a people in God's Word and the World is sending over missiles! Disease and sinful attitudes and a plethora of counseling issues fire at you even as you seek to teach the people God's way. It seems as soon as you get a program going that will result in discipleship, Satan or the world or the flesh throws another grenade at you! Soldiering is hard work and so is pastoring! My dearly beloved, in case you haven't figured it out yet, if you aren't careful this can make you look like a fool! Crawling around on a beach avoiding fire while trying to secure a beachhead is not usually done with a lot of grace and finesse! and I can assure you that trying to bring the Gospel to a community while being ambushed at every move by Satan can also make you look less than professional at times! My dear friends, you very well know that you can lose your jobs trying to advance the Word of God in our day to a people who might have come to the place where they enjoy the sins that you are exposing!

Thank God, though, that we have the right weaponry: The Word of God!

Praise be to Christ that our victory is sure in the Sovereign hand of Almighty God!

Glory be to the Lord that the Commander in Chief of our Army is the Lord God of Hosts and every enemy shall fall before His Mighty Plan is finished!

But, just in case you are more concerned about your career than your calling, let me suggest a few steps to help you:

(1) IDENTIFY DIFFICULTIES BEFORE THEY CONFRONT YOU.

By identifying the fact that a given course of action could result in possible danger to your career, you can easily avoid crushing defeat by just avoiding the territory altogether. For instance, if you haven't gathered this by now, by avoiding any teaching on financial stewardship you can avoid a whole host of difficulties.

(2) STEER CLEAR OF DIFFICULT PEOPLE.

The second way to avoid a problem in your career is to do as one church consultant I heard said to do: "Choose who you lose." That is, identify those people who are difficult and get rid of them. Force them to leave, somehow, so you don't have to minister to them. Never mind that their behavior may be concealing deep pain; let another minister who doesn't have a professional image to uphold deal with them!

(3) AVOID STANDING FOR WHAT COULD VERY WELL CAUSE YOU TO LOSE SLEEP.

This third way of doing it the easy way is designed to get the most out of life! When you consider that the value of a good night's sleep is worth more than getting involved with sleep depriving, difficult issues such as figuring out how to minister to the handicapped in your community and how to reach the unchurched in the two mile area around your church, you will soon be on your way to a more professional image. After all, baggy eyes and a wrinkled brow don't do anything for your photo in the community news section of the local paper!

II. YOU CAN LOSE YOUR MINISTRY AND EXCEL IN YOUR PROFESSION IF YOU WILL JUST DO IT THE POPULAR WAY. (V. 4)

The Apostle tells us that

> No one serving as a soldier gets involved in civilian
> affairs—he wants to please his commanding officer.
> (2 Timothy 2.4, NIV)

The minister of the Gospel, the Church leader, every Christian in whatever place God has called them, must have a single-mindedness about his or her duty to carry out the Great Commission. He says here that our motivation is to please God. That is what Paul is saying. "Timothy, there are many lures out there which can rob you of your priorities as a pastor and one of them is to seek to please others. Do not yield to the temptation. When you pastor, dear boy, you are to do so with an eye on pleasing God."

Now, I'm going to tell you a story if you promise not to tell anyone else. When I was playing baseball as a boy in little league, I had a great coach. I would do anything to please that man. When I was in center field and a pop fly came to me, I would run and catch it and then I would just look over to "Mr. Sonny" and look for his approval. One day, I knew there was a girl from my class sitting in the bleachers. Now, this girl was a beauty. She was clearly out of my league, I thought, but if I could just "wow" her with my athletic prowess, I could get her attention. Pleasing her (and of course, she had no idea who I was and I subsequently proved that she didn't care) was the only thing I could think of when another ball was hit in my direction. I was going to have to dive for the ball to catch it (but what a wonderful opportunity to impress that gal!). So, I did and I barely caught it, but I nabbed it like a pro! I came up and with great dramatic flair raised the ball in the air to show her and everyone one else that I had miraculously caught it! The problem was in the midst of my grand performance, the man on third tagged up and with me taking a bow in the outfield, he trotted on into home plate and scored the winning run. "Mr. Sonny", my coach, got real angry. He benched me. and the girl left the game to get a snow cone and never saw my performance anyway.

Isn't that the way it is in the ministry? We seek to do it the popular way when God tells us to do it His way. Paul says we are to please our Commander, not the civilian world! In preparing our sermons, are we seeking to please God or show off the fact that we know Greek? When we sign up for our doctoral courses, are we seeking to become educated in order to please God or to impress the next pulpit committee? When we show up at the bedside of our church leader's wives, are we there to communicate the love and healing of Christ to hurting people, or to show our church leaders, finally, just how hard we work? When we get an opportunity to preach to our peers, do we do it to "wow" them or just to be obedient to the One who has called us to preach?

Too often, we have made a decision in the ministry that we hoped would make us look good to a watching world, only to disregard God's plan for our ministries. It's a wonder He doesn't bench us all!

By His grace, may we resolve this day to work as unto the Lord and not unto men.

Of course, we can disregard the Apostle's Spirit-inspired words here, and do it the popular way. How is that?

(1) IMPRESS YOUR PEERS

We all want to be admired. Why not use churches as stepping stones to get that perfect pulpit which will make everyone else envious! It will be obvious to all then of your natural abilities. Some may even believe that you are God's greatest gift to your denomination and the next superstar!

(2) PATRONIZE YOUR PARISHIONERS

Of course, you must do this one! With just a little reading on Machiavellian technique, all of us can learn how to make our parishioners feel better about themselves, enough to leave us alone so we can spend time doing whatever it is we really want to do!

(3) PLEASE POTENTIAL MEMBERS

We all know that you won't find anyone admitting this in a church growth manual, but, hey, we're all professionals here, right? Avoid the sinner stuff, get around those pesky vows of membership and just make them feel that as long as they keep their pet sins private, we're not concerned about them.

But, then again, there is that tricky little statement in 2 Timothy 2.4:

> No one serving as a soldier gets involved in civilian affairs—he wants to please his commanding officer.
> (2 Timothy 2.4, NIV)

III. YOU CAN LOSE YOUR MINISTRY AND STILL EXCEL IN YOUR PROFESSION IF YOU WILL ONLY DO IT YOUR WAY! (V. 5)

Verse five says:

> Similarly, if anyone competes as an athlete, he does not receive the victor's crown unless he competes according to the rules. (2 Timothy 2.5, NIV)

The notes to the old Geneva Bible on this verse provide our interpretation:

> The ministry is similar to a game in which men strive for the victory, and no man is crowned, unless he strive according to the laws which are prescribed, be they ever so hard and painful.

All of you Olympic buffs, answer me this: What do the Olympic committees do with people who win foot races while on performance enhancing drugs? That happened just a few years ago in Seoul, South Korea. What happens to a weight lifter on steroids? Of course, their victory is ruled ineligible. They are dismissed from the games under a cloud of shame. They could have been crowned with garland and a gold medal. Instead they are remembered as phonies and as disgraces to their countries.

The rules of ministry are easy. Carry out your charge, whatever it is, in spirit and in truth with an eye for God's glory. That means different things to different people. For the church planter, it means establishing your church upon God's Word, not upon gimmicks and easy steps to success. For the pastor, it means building ministries that will reach the lost and edify the saints—not just quick fixes to prop you up until you can advance to your next pastorate. For the church leader, it may mean actually getting involved with helping to shepherd the flock rather than just acting as an occasional glorified business consultant.

Naturally, this way of doing things can cost you dearly and even rob you of your professional image. But, if you chose to forego doing it God's Way, you will actually lose your ministry. You will miss the crown, which He will give to His faithful servants on that Day when He judges the living and the dead. Isn't it much better to labor and toil for the prize and go to sleep at night knowing you are on the right track, no matter how difficult, than to do it your way?

But for those of you intent on doing it your way, here, again, are some pragmatic tips for a sure-fire victory in the ministry:

(1) THINK OF YOURSELF AS THE FIRST ONE TO EVER DO IT.

Translation: church history is not for you! This is the Twenty-first Century and you are in control of your own success or failure.

(2) AVOID THE COUNSEL OF OTHERS.

After all, they are not responsible for building your nest egg. How will you make it up the ladder, if you have pious friends warning you against what will obviously place you above them? Forget them! Aren't you doing this for your families' benefit?

(3) RATIONALIZE AWAY EXAMPLES OF HOW GOD'S SERVANTS IN THE BIBLE DID IT.

If your conscience bothers you after reading of how Joseph did it God's Way rather than his way and yet still came out on top, then just consider that Joseph never got an article on "Career Management" published in his denominational magazine either!

But, I must call you back to these words:

> Similarly, if anyone competes as an athlete, he does not receive the victor's crown unless he competes according to the rules. (2 Timothy 2.5, NIV)

IV. YOU CAN LOSE YOUR MINISTRY WHILE EXCELLING IN YOUR PROFESSION IF YOU DO IT THE LEAST MESSY WAY (THAT IS WITHOUT GETTING TOO INVOLVED...) (VV. 6-10)

I come to my final point and it is concerned most of all with our degree of involvement in the lives of others.

Listen to verse 10,

> Therefore I endure everything for the sake of the elect, that they too may obtain the salvation that is in Christ Jesus, with eternal glory. (2 Timothy 2.10, NIV)

I must admit that I can imagine Paul saying that he would endure all for the sake of the glory of Jesus Christ! I can expect the great Apostle to admit that the cause of the Gospel motivates him to endure all things! I can believe that Paul would say that he will undergo persecution for the honor of God...but, it is shocking for me to hear him say that "I endure everything for the sake of the elect."

I am startled because I know that people can hurt you in the ministry. I know because I think it is true that people can use you in the ministry. I am not naturally given to give up everything for such people. I am not even inclined to give up much for people who like me, much less than people who use me! I am hard-pressed to suffer for my own relatives, much less for nations and regions and peoples that have nothing even closely related to my life! But that is what Paul is saying. His ministry is driven by sacrificial love for others; that they might obtain eternal life in Jesus Christ.

Now, let me stick my clerical tongue-in-cheek for one final admonition.

Dear friends, this is perhaps the greatest risk to your career. To give your life for evil men—well, it will ruin you! To risk your professional image on people who could never appreciate your homiletic brilliance or your keen perception of the flow of history or your scholarly grasp of Hebrew syntax is to "cast your pearls before swine!" Come and let us reason together and let me show you how to keep your professional image secure:

(1) DO MINISTRY WITHOUT GETTING INVOLVED WITH PEOPLE

Most people have not been to seminary and do not understand the real issues in the life of a church. Skip them and you can manage your future much easier and a whole lot quicker.

(2) DO MINISTRY WITHOUT GETTING INVOLVED WITH THEIR PROBLEMS

Can you imagine how far you can go if you don't have to spend your emotional energies on couples facing divorce or singles facing loneliness issues or people struggling to understand what you mean when you preach...?

DOCTORS OR HEALERS?

O.K. No more funny business. This is, quite obviously, just the opposite of what Paul is saying when he says he "endures all for the sake of the elect." But, does his statement really characterize your understanding of your ministry?

You and I know that there is a temptation to define success in a way that is just the opposite of what God requires for our ministry. and you and I know that one can do it and still get nominated for Clergyman of the Year!

But such success comes at a high price.

It is time for my little exercise to come to an end. Let me get very serious in closing.

I saw a movie the other day that centered on the life of a medical school community. It involved a young man who was struggling with his call to become a physician. At the end of the movie there was a quote which really grabbed me. The quote was this:

> I made doctors, but people need healers.

It grabbed my heart because it was spoken by a Medical School Faculty member who in dealing with her own inoperable and terminal disease, found that the very men she had trained were quite professional, but without the slightest evidence of compassion for her as a suffering patient. She looked at one of those young men who were struggling with his call to be a doctor. It was that woman, that faculty member, who told a young medical student, "I made doctors, but people need healers." When she spoke those poignant words, she seem to be telling him, "Don't be just another professional physician...they lack the heart and soul that is truly needed by a patient who is gripped by fear of the unknown and who is placing her life in his hands! Be a healer! Have a heart for your patients! Show us that we are not just another manila folder in your clinical file cabinet!"

> I made doctors, but people need healers.

I looked at my life and my ministry. I was growing in my profession while all the while possibly distancing myself from the real-life pains of my people. I was diagnosing their spiritual conditions without weeping for them. I was getting professional without heart.

> Some of us are clergymen, but people need healers.
>
> Others of us are professional board members of the church, but people need care givers.

How different we often are from the Apostle Paul who said, "I endure all things for the sake of the elect, that they also may obtain the salvation which is in Christ Jesus..." What beatings and insults and deprivation of every human comfort was Paul's for the sake of other people! Paul was imitating Christ who said He came to serve and to give His life as a ransom for many! and he tells us in Philippians that we must imitate Jesus Christ! Our Lord left his royal robes of heaven to come and take on the poverty stricken conditions of a carpenter in an occupied country. He offered His Body and His Blood as a sacrifice of unimaginable Love for a people who were sinners and who even hated Him to death!

You can be a raging success and still lose your passion for souls, which is your ministry.

Of course, you will never be happy. Of course, you will one day die and have to face the truth that it was not worth it! Of course, you will regret not having given your all to the ministry to which Almighty God had called you! For if God has called you to be an ambassador for His Kingdom and to plead with the hearts and minds of men to embrace Jesus Christ, you will never be happy until your life is in every way poured out as an offering for the sake of God's elect.

Dearest fellow labors in Christ, please go ahead and commit yourself to improving your ministry. Become a sharper instrument in the Hands of Him who called you. But do it while getting your hands dirty in the rich soil of human lives which are in desperate need of someone like you who are willing to love them and help them to,

> Obtain the salvation which is in Christ Jesus with eternal glory.

Seek God's forgiveness if you have failed. Receive your renewal in Him and recover your passion for the ministry to which God has called you. Do it right now before you go any further in this day.

In the Name of the Father and of the Son and of the Holy Spirit. Amen.

THE JUSTIFICATION OF PREACHING

VALIDATING OUR IDENTITY

Here is a simple portion of Scripture, yet I would say it is a very profound portion which cries out to be heard today—by laymen, yes—but especially by those who are called to imitate our Master in the preaching task:

> and Jesus went about all
> Galilee...preaching...(from Matthew 4.23,
> KJV)

"CAN WE JUSTIFY PREACHING?"

John Stott has remarked that "Preaching is indispensable to Christianity. Without preaching a necessary part of its authenticity is lost."[45] Robert Rayburn, the founder of Covenant Theological Seminary and Covenant College, believed that preaching was so important that it must occupy first place in the studies of seminarians after the study of Christ, Himself. Of the study of preaching, Rayburn stated:

> Christ is the only king of your studies, but homiletics is the queen.[46]

D. James Kennedy, in his retiring Moderator's address at the 1989 General Assembly of the Presbyterian Church in America, charged the teaching elders of that Assembly with the words from an old pastor:

> Why stoop to be a king...when you've been called to preach?[47]

---

[45] John R. Stott, Between Two Worlds (Eerdmans, 1982), 15.

[46] Quoted in Bryan Chapell, Christ-centered Preaching (Baker, 1994), 17.

[47] Private notes from the General Assembly of the PCA, Los Angeles, CA, 1989

These are lofty remarks. If they are true, then actually preaching is the cornerstone of our ministry. Preaching, therefore, is the very center of our ministry (some would say along with the emblems of the Word: the Sacraments)[48] and, therefore, the study of preaching is central to our ministry. But, there are skeptics abounding, both in the world and even in the Church. David Martin Lloyd-Jones, in his lectures at Westminster Seminary in the early part of the 1970s, aware then of the skeptics, asked a very fundamental question in order to address the issue:

Can we justify preaching?[49]

In other words, can we really make such high and holy pronouncements about preaching? Can we justify this course? Can we make sense out of calling young men from a life of engineering or business or politics or science into a life of preaching? Those are all productive occupations. They are measurable in their contributions to the market (the Temple of our culture), but preaching? Can we justify the expense of seminaries and the efforts of professors and staff to recruit and train preachers? Can we justify paying a preacher's salary? I once had an officer in my church tell me that "All you do is give a 'speech' a couple of times a week and we pay you all of this money and all of this vacation. It sounds like a good deal to me—where do we sign up?" There was much laughter around the table. Even officers in the church who have been taught the centrality of the Word become skeptics of preaching. There are other questions, though, in this matter. Can we build churches, designed with pulpits at their center, just to gather and hear preachers preach? Can we support global missions in which we send preacher families away to foreign lands... just to preach?

There are many that would say it is a joke. I fear that there are many who would say that the days in which we live, and the people to whom we must minister, require that we forget preaching and preachers.

Can we justify preaching?

---

[48] A Minister of Word and Sacrament seems to be a good phrase upon examination of the preacher's duties from Scripture. Yet, the Sacraments are always tied to the Word. Preaching, then, might be said to have the authoritative position between the two.

[49] David Martin Lloyd-Jones, "Preaching and Preachers (Zondervan, 1971). 10.

NO. PREACHING IS ANACHRONISTIC

Many view preaching as being old fashioned. "We live in a day of 'high-tech.' We must reach modern man with the delivery systems to which he is accustomed as well as the delivery style to which he responds so naturally. Thus, we do not need preachers, per se, but could do better with delivery systems such as e-mail, fax, television, radio, and multi-media presentations. Thus, we do not need sermons with their emphasis upon the written Word of God. We would do better with dramas, in which real people just like us give us brief snapshots of ourselves and our everyday dilemmas happily (and quickly, please) leading to a spectacular and entertaining host of a light-hearted, cheerful, encouraging 7-step principles for living. Sermons are out. Preachers are out. It cannot be justified in today's world."

I have in my study a photograph of Dr. David Martin Lloyd-Jones. He is sitting gravely and seriously in his book-lined study as Westminster Chapel in London. Attired in his black pulpit robe and his right hand on the Bible, the picture reminds me of the weighty matter of preaching. It beckons to me, as a preacher, to remember the study and seriousness that is required to carry on the ministry of preaching. Well, I once had a visitor to my study who was a child. The child saw the picture of Martin Lloyd-Jones and asked, "Who is that old man?" That was an innocent question from a child, but it is an adequate portrayal of the world and the modern Church looking at the classic model of preaching and asking, "Who is that old man?"

That picture of preaching as the Church has known it for centuries is as out of date in the minds of some today as a Model-T Ford. You have all heard the automobile advertising jingle that goes, "This is not your father's Oldsmobile." "What is needed today," these folks insist, "is a new ministry—one that speaks to the post-modern man in his language and in his way. Make preaching light and make it brief and keep your thoughts on this life only."

Preaching cannot be justified in this view. Seminary education as we know it throughout the history of the church is no longer needed because the classical model always sought to train men in the "Queen of studies," homiletics, and prepare them for a life of preaching. A weighty study of homiletics—of studying preaching—its theological ground, its glorious history, its finest masters is, to the modern skeptic, is like running a trade school in the year 2001 to educate future mechanics how to work on 1940

Oldsmobiles! So, homiletics and preaching are, sadly, being replaced in many seminaries with courses in communication.

There is, of course much to substantiate their position. Note Neil Postman's books like Technopoly and Amusing Ourselves to Death.[50] These poignantly, and I believe correctly, point out that we are in a post-typographical age and a post-oratorical age. David Wells, in his God in the Wasteland, does the same and applies his findings to the Church. Os Guinness summed it up when he looked at the effect of popular culture on public discourse. He describes the shift from

> word to image, action to spectacle, exposition to entertainment, truth to feeling...conviction to sentiment and authoritative utterance to discussion and sharing.[51]

We live in the day of communication through technology. A preacher standing in a pulpit with a Bible delivering a message from the Bible seems archaic in this view.

Douglas D. Webster in his insightful volume called Selling Jesus: What's Wrong with Marketing the Church understands the phenomena of which I speak when he quotes a modern preaching skeptic. Of course, the skeptic is a modern-day preacher:

> When I preach, [wrote the clerical skeptic] I figure
> I have about one or two minutes for people to
> decide if they want to listen to me or not.

He compensates for this pressure by selecting his sermon topics from the self-help section in the local bookstore and surveying people in his church for pressing needs. These have included the following:

1. How can I have a happier marriage?

2. How can I handle my money better?

---

[50] Neil Postman, Amusing Ourselves to Death: Public Discourse in the Age of Show business (Penguin Books, 1985).

[51] Os Guinness, "Mission in the Face of Modernity," in The Gospel in the Modern World: A Tribute to John Stott, ed. Martyn Eden and David F. Wells (InterVarsity Press) 1991, 95.

3. I don't like my job. What can I do about it?

4. How do I get guidance about my employment?

5. Will I be caught in an ACOA (adult children of alcoholics) pattern all my life?

6. How did we get the Bible? How do I know it's God's Word?

7. How can I be a better parent?

8. How can I get more time for myself?

9. How can I feel better about myself?

Besides "how-to-" sermons with practical "take-away" points, this modern minister advises pastors,

> Limit your preaching to roughly 20 minutes, because boomers don't have much time to spare. and don't forget to keep your messages light and informal, liberally sprinkling them with humor and personal anecdotes.[52]

This is what I am talking about. Preaching, "like all forms of instruction, faces increasing pressure to accommodate itself to an audience shaped by television."[53] Preaching (like Worship) must be, to borrow Marva Dawn's phrase, "dumbed down" in order to be relevant.[54]

Have you noticed the trends in pulpit architecture? The reality that I speak of is reflected perfectly in the changes that have occurred in the physical pulpit itself! Rarely in new church design (particularly in evangelical churches) will you find the heavy, old oak pulpits of our older church buildings. Plexiglas podiums have replaced the great wooden pulpits. What a metaphor for the evolution (downward evolution) of preaching! Preaching is no longer heavy,

---

[52] Douglas D. Webster, Selling Jesus: What's Wrong with Marketing the Church (InterVarsity Press, 1992), 82-83. Webster is quoting from Doug Murren, The Baby Boomerang (Regal, 1990), 101.

[53] Ibid. 84.

[54] Marva J. Dawn, Reaching Out Without Dumbing Down: A Theology of Worship for the Turn-Of-The-Century Culture (Eerdmans, 1995).

permanent, serious, sober, urgent, deep and doctrinally rich; it is transparent, light, inoffensive, and easily moveable.

Of course, God makes OAK. Man makes PLEXIGLAS. Plexiglas preachers and Plexiglas preaching reminds me of J. Vernon McGee's wonderful and witty descriptive phrase of this very thing.

> ...preacher-ettes giving sermon-ettes to Christian-ettes.

We have established, then, that some today believe that preaching cannot be justified. It is anachronistic.

Consider another major category with me. Some will say:

NO. WE CANNOT JUSTIFY PREACHING. THERE ARE OTHER MORE PRESSING NEEDS IN THE CHURCH

Preaching cannot be justified as the "Queen of our studies" when there are more pressing needs in the Church. I shall deal with three of these.

EMOTIONAL WORSHIP

The matter of entertainment in worship has been alluded to. I believe that preaching is not justified, as we understand it in Scripture, when one believes that the best way to reach a person is through creating an atmosphere of a heightened emotional state.

Now, let me explain. When I say, "emotional worship," I am referring broadly to the contemporary movement of Praise and Worship services as well as to "revivalist" services which still predominate many fundamentalist circles. I know that some of you probably go to these and I affirm that these are helping people in a number of ways. Indeed, not a few of those churches that employ such music have produced good preaching. But, by and far, the movement has de-emphasized a classical approach to preaching (and when I say classical I mean to say the majority approach taken to preaching in Protestant churches for 400 years).

Central to emotional worship services is "producing the atmosphere"[55] for a person to "make a decision for Christ." The idea seems to be to use rhythmic music to break down emotional walls and allow the words of the Gospel to go to the heart. The problem

---

[55] Lloyd-Jones, Preachers and Preaching, 17.

IDENTITY

with it is that it takes precedence over preaching in many cases. Music controls these services, not preaching and its companion—the Sacraments. All of the energy of the church, a great deal of personnel of the church and no small amount of money is spent to create and promote a "quality" contemporary music feast. Or, in the case of more fundamentalist churches, a "song leader" is a "new kind of official in the church"[56] who conducts the singing and is supposed to get the people charged up. Preaching is de-emphasized. Why? Whether they have stated it or not, they have determined that they cannot justify their existence with "just preaching." They need more. They need music. They need to get the people emotionally ready to hear the Word.

LITURGICAL RENEWAL

On the other hand, there has in recent years been a revival of interest in liturgy. This is very good in many cases. We recall, however, the warning by Martyn Lloyd-Jones who declared that "...as preaching has waned, there has been an increase in the formal element in the service."[57]

While the emotional worship crowd cannot justify preaching as central because of a prioritized emphasis upon emotionally charged music, this movement replaces preaching with form and order and set prayers at it's center.

We neither reject liturgy or emotion. But, we plead for the primacy of preaching. Alas, however, there is a growing trend to replace Word with form and call it renewal. Preaching, as it has been known in Protestantism is rejected.

EGALITARIANISM

Another movement that deliberately de-emphasizes classical preaching is egalitarianism. This movement is a reaction against clericalism—the idea that the hierarchy of the Church dominates the Church, and the Layman is relegated to a second-class position. Egalitarianism, though, moves from one extreme to another, denying the place of ordained ministry in the order of the Church. Thus, in that system of thought, anyone can administer the

---

[56] Ibid.

[57] Ibid. 16.

sacrament and anyone can preach and anyone can lead worship. The Scriptures declare that only some are called to ruling and teaching offices in the Church (see my lecture on Vocation) and that such offices carry with them peculiar responsibilities. One of those is to preach the Word of God as an ambassador of Jesus Christ under the license of other leaders in the Church. Egalitarianism has often been observed in the "house church" movement and in certain "Bible" churches and "New Testament" churches.

Preaching is not justified in egalitarianism even though the order of services may place priority upon preaching. Egalitarianism denies the ordained role of the preacher and turns preaching into Bible Studies, admonitions, warnings, and other "good" practices in and of themselves. The problem is that preaching is connected to a preacher. Someone is called to preach and others are called to heed and practice.

CONCLUSION

The question had been put:

Can we justify preaching?

Many answer "no".

But, notice, please, that their answers are based upon expediency, logic or "what seems right." We cannot justify preaching on anecdotal evidences.

There is only one place to go to justify preaching: to the Sender of Preachers and the Great Preacher, Himself: Our Lord Jesus Christ.

WHAT PREACHING IS NOT

We might continue our study by pointing out misunderstandings that some have about preaching. This sort of preaching can not be justified from God's Word.

ORATORICAL DEMONSTRATION

There is in the Church a wrong understanding of preaching that associates it with fine oratory. It is style for style's sake. It is the mastering of public communication techniques. In former days, it was called "conceits." It is flowery a message designed to emotionally thrill you or put you in awe of the messenger's rhetorical abilities. It is not a preacher "preaching...because [he] is busting with truths which could not help finding expression, but because [he is the] master of fine phrases..."[58]

Rhetoric may be employed. Oratorical skills of the likes of Apollos are to be valued in the Church, but preaching is not this alone.

TEACHING

I strongly believe there is a fine line that separates the act of teaching and the act of preaching.

In St. Matthew 4.23, our Lord Jesus went about both teaching and preaching. We must not ever divorce the reality of teaching from the ministry of the Church, and we must not discount the teaching element in preaching. But, preaching is not simply teaching. Jesus was a teacher, but He came preaching, as well. He taught about the nature of the Kingdom of God and He proclaimed that it had come. There is an authority and urgency and a call for change in preaching that is not necessarily there in teaching.

There is a Greek word for teaching: didasko—to teach—and one for preaching: kerysso—to proclaim. The sacred act of preaching—the Kerygma—is our concern.

It is, I think, a matter of emphasis and objective. The emphasis of teaching is on the communication and conveyance of information of one sort or another. The object of teaching is to impart that information to the student in such a way that he or she recalls it and can utilize it in his or her endeavors. The emphasis of preaching, though, is redemption for fallen man through repentance of sin and faith in the risen Lord Jesus Christ. St. Paul sums up this whole message in four words: the Cross of Christ. (I Cor. 1.17). The objective is to bring transformation to the human condition by calling for repentance and faith in Jesus Christ and offering redemption in Him. This happens in an evangelistic service in one way and in pastoral preaching in quite another way, but the emphasis is always redemption and the objective is always transformation.

Now, there is a misunderstanding of these principles which works its way out in various forms. Some approach the pulpit as simply a

---

[58] See Lloyd-Jones' quotation of Edward Hatch on page 14 of Preachers and Preaching

teacher. Often times the messages become just essays. They have been carefully prepared on paper and come across as such. It lacks urgency. Lloyd-Jones said a sermon is "doctrine on fire" and that is it. It is teaching that is blazing with a supernatural mandate from God. Manuscripts must blaze with unction!

MOTIVATIONAL TALKS

I heard of an Easter sermon preached by someone entitled "You Can't Keep a Good Man Down." Now, that is a catchy title and it seems to offer motivational help for those trapped in a suburban rat race. I never read or heard the message so I will withhold comments on it, but its title at least illustrates my point here.

Preaching is not a locker room pep talk. It's not a weekly inspirational injection to prop up soul-weary warriors, though it may have some of those elements. It is more. It is the announcement of Good News and the application of God's Word, some of it motivational and some of it downright depressing (you are a sinner and will die in your sins if you do not repent!).

Preaching is scandalous. It is, as St. Paul said, "foolishness" to a watching world.

> For we preach Christ crucified, to the Jews a stumbling block and to the Greeks foolishness. (I Cor. 1.23)

Our message is foolish and so is our occupation.

We can only justify preaching by appealing to the One who calls preachers: God. For preaching is, as Dr. Robert Reymond has called it, " A Word from Another World."

We justify preaching, then, only from God's word, the Bible. Then we shall come to see why Lloyd-Jones could say,

> To me the work of preaching is the highest and greatest and the most glorious calling to which anyone can ever be called.[59]

and we shall be able to affirm the words of Dr. Kennedy:

---

[59] From the cover of Preachers and Preaching

> Why stoop to be a king when you have been called to preach.

WHAT PREACHING IS

PREACHING MUST BE OF NECESSITY DEFINED BY GOD HIMSELF

I will begin this portion of the lecture by stating that God alone defines preaching. Jesus was a preacher. He sent out preachers. He called preachers, and we believe that He still calls preachers. Preaching is a Word from Another World. It is God's message to men through His inerrant and infallible Word. We must therefore understand preaching in light of what the Bible says about it. We continue to ask the Question: "Can we justify preaching?" We cannot do it from the world and trends in the Church. We go to the Bible.

> The authority of preaching is not heightened but lost if the preacher forsakes his place behind the Book.[60]

THE OLD TESTAMENT WITNESS TO PREACHING

Edmund Clowney states that

> The ministry of the word springing from God's manifold revelation is twofold: first, there is a prophetic, mediatorial ministry of conveying God's words to people... [and]...The second aspect of the ministry of the word is the teaching of the revealed word.[61]

PREACHING AS THE PROPHETIC UTTERANCE

The inscription of the Word of God began with Moses receiving the revelation of God and bringing it to the people (Exod. 20.19[62]:

---

[60] Edmund Clowney, Preaching and Biblical Theology (Presbyterian and Reformed), 61.

[61] Ibid. 48,49.

[62] "And they said unto Moses, Speak thou with us, and we will hear; but let not God speak with us, lest we die." (Exodus 20.19, KJV).

Deut. 5.27-33[63]). Moses possessed a mediatorial function in the community of faith—declaring the Word of God to the people. The people were sinful and required special messengers from God—prophets—who would proclaim God's revelation to them. These prophets were precursors of the Prophet who would be a greater Moses:

> I will raise them up a Prophet from among their brethren, like unto thee, and will put my words in his mouth; and he shall speak unto them all that I shall command him. (Deuteronomy 18.18, KJV)

The prophets were preachers. Preaching the Word of God directly from God is how the Bible came to be. While there are no more prophets (Heb. 1.1[64]), and the Prophet has come—even our Lord

---

[63] "Go thou near, and hear all that the Lord our God shall say; and speak thou unto us all that the Lord our God shall peak unto thee; and we will hear [it], and do [it]. And the Lord heard the voice of your words, when ye spake unto me; and the Lord said unto me, I have heard the voice of the words of this people, which they have spoken unto thee: they have well said all that they have spoken. O that there were such an heart in them, that they would fear me, and keep all my commandments always, that it might be well with them, and with their children forever! Go say to them, Get you into your tents again. But as for thee, stand thou here by me, and I will speak unto thee all the commandments, and the statutes, and the judgments, which thou shalt teach them, that the Lord your God hath commanded you; ye shall not turn aside to the right hand or to the left. Ye shall walk in all the ways which the Lord your God hath commanded you, that ye may live, and [that it may be] well with you and [that] ye may prolong [your] days in the land which ye shall possess." (Deuteronomy 5.27-33, KJV)

[64] "Charity never faileth but whether [there be] prophecies, they shall fail; whether [there be] tongues, they shall cease; whether [there be] knowledge, it shall vanish away. For we know in part, and we prophesy in part. But when that which is perfect is come, then that which is in part shall be done away." (1 Corinthians 13.8-10, KJV). "And he gave some evangelists; and some, pastors and teachers;" (Ephesians 4.11, KJV). "God, who at sundry times and in divers manners spake in time past unto the fathers by the prophets, Hath in these last days spoken unto us by [his] son, whom he hath appointed heir of all things, by whom also he made the worlds;" (Hebrews 1.1,2, KJV). "We have also a more sure word of prophecy; where unto ye do well that ye take heed, as unto a light that shineth in a dark place, until the day dawn, and the day star arise in your hearts: Knowing that first, that no prophesy of the scripture is of any private interpretation. For the prophecy came not in old time by the will of man: but holy men of God spake [as they were] moved by the Holy Ghost." (2 Peter 1.19-21, KJV). "For I testify unto every man that heareth the words of the prophesy of

Jesus Christ—every preacher is yet a prophet in the sense that he is God's ambassador to a given people and he carries with him a great message from the King.[65]

PREACHING AS EXPLANATION AND APPLICATION OF SCRIPTURE

The revealed Word having come to the people, God caused preachers to expound that Word.

There is no greater example of this than the preaching of Ezra the Priest. Clowney calls his ministry,

> ...the crowning example of the faithful discharge of this aspect of the ministry of the word in the Old Testament. It became the model for synagogue preaching, and our Lord followed the pattern in Nazareth when he proclaimed the fulfillment of Isaiah's prophesy in himself (Luke 4.16-21)[66]

Let us look, then, at that passage in Nehemiah 8 at that account. The passage is easily divided the following way:

1. The Assembling of the Covenant Community

---

this book, If any man shall add unto these things, God shall add unto him the plagues that are written in this book: And if any man shall take away from the words of the book of this prophesy, God shall take away his part out of the book of life, and out of the holy city, and [from] the things which are written in this book." (Revelation 22.18-19, KJV).

[65] "Now then we are ambassadors for Christ, as though God did beseech [you] by us: we pray [you] in Christ's stead, be ye reconciled to God." (2 Corinthians 5.20, KJV).

[66] "And he came to Nazareth where he had been brought up: and, as his custom was, he went into the synagogue on the Sabbath day, and stood up for to read. And there was delivered unto him the book of the prophet Isaiah. And when he had opened the book, he found the place where it was written. The Spirit of the Lord [is] upon me, because he hath anointed me to preach the gospel to the poor; he hath sent me to heal the brokenhearted, to preach deliverance to the captives, and recovering of sight to the blind, to set at liberty them that are bruised, To preach the acceptable year of the Lord. And he closed the book, and he gave [it] again to the minister, and sat down. And the eyes of all them that were in the synagogue were fastened on him. And he began to say unto them, this day is this scripture fulfilled in you your ears." (Luke 4.16-21, KJV).

and all the people gathered themselves together as one man in to the street that [was] before the water gate; (Nehemiah 8.1a, KJV)

2. The Covenant Community's Call to the Preacher (1b)

and they spake unto Ezra the scribe to bring the book of the law of Moses, which the Lord had commanded to Israel. (Nehemiah 8.1b, KJV)

3. The Processional (2)

and Ezra the priest brought the law before the congregation both of men and women, and all that could hear with understanding, upon the first day of the seventh month. (Nehemiah 8.2, KJV)

4. The Reading of the Word of God (3)

and he read therein before the street that [was] before the water gate from the morning until midday, before the men and the women, and those that could understand; and the ears of all the people [were attentive] unto the book of the law. (Nehemiah 8.3, KJV)

5. The Preparation of the Covenant Community to Hear the Word of God (4-6).

and Ezra the scribe stood upon a pulpit of wood, which they had made for the purpose; and beside him stood Mattithiah, and Shema, and Anaiah, and Urijah, and Hilkiah, and Maaseiah, an his right hand; and on his left hand, Pedaiah, and Mishael, and Malchiah, and Hashum, and Hashbadana, Zechariah, [and] Meshullam. and Ezra opened the book in the sight of all the people; for he was above all the people; and when he opened it, all the people stood up: and Ezra blessed the Lord, the great God. and all the people answered, Amen, Amen, with lifting up their hands: and they bowed their heads, and worshipped the Lord with [their] faces to the ground. (Nehemiah 8.4-6, KJV)

IDENTITY

6. The Proclamation, Explanation and Application of the Word of God (7-8)

> Also, Jeshua, and Bani, and Sherbiah, Jamin, Akkup, Shabbethai, Hodijah, Maaseiah, Kelita, Azariah, Jozabad, Hanan, Pelaiah, and the Levites, caused the people to understand the law: and the people [stood] in their place. So they read in the book in the law of God distinctly, and gave the sense, and caused [them] to understand the reading. (Nehemiah 8.7-8, KJV)

7. The Benediction and Dismissal (9, 10, 11)

> and Nehemiah, which [is] the Tirshatha, and Ezra the priest the scribe, and the Levites that taught the people, said unto all the people, This day [is] holy unto the Lord your God; mourn not, nor weep. For all the people wept, when they heard the words of the law. Then he said unto them, Go your way, eat the fat, and drink the sweet, and send portions unto them for whom nothing is prepared: for [this] day [is] holy unto our Lord; neither be ye sorry; for the joy of the Lord is your strength. So the Levites stilled all the people, saying, Hold your peace, for the day [is] holy; neither be ye grieved. (Nehemiah 8.9-11,KJV)

8. The Covenant Community's Response (12)

> and all the people went their way to eat, and to drink, and to send portions, and to make great mirth, because they had understood the words that were declared unto them. (Nehemiah 8.12, KJV)

Verse 8 says in the New King James, "they gave the sense, and helped them to understand."

Here is the second task of preaching: to be God's ordained representative to "open up" the Scriptures for the people of God and help them to apply it.

It occurs to me as I read this passage that the work of preaching is intimately (but we understand not necessarily) wed to the pastorate. Ezra, with the assistance of the Elders and the Levites (the Elders and the Deacons or the Vestry and the Diaconate or the Deacons or the Stewards) carried on a pastoral ministry of teaching the people privately what had been preached in public service. This is the whole matter that is taken up in Richard Baxter's The Reformed Pastor. You'll not get out of this seminary without reading that one, but I want to give you other thoughtful words on this subject from Phillips Brooks, in his famous 1877 Yale's Lectures on Preaching gave the following analysis of preaching and pastoral work:

> ...the work of the preacher and the pastor really belong together, and ought not to be separated. I believe that very strongly. Every now and then somebody rises with a plea that is very familiar and specious. He says, how much better it would be if only there could be a classification of ministers and duties. Let some ministers be wholly preachers and some be wholly pastors. Let one class visit the flock, to direct and comfort them; and the other class stand in the pulpit. You will not go far in the ministry before you are tempted to echo that desire. The two parts of a preacher's work are always in rivalry. When you find that you can never sit down to study and write without the faces of the people, who you know need your care, looking at you from the paper; and yet you can never go out among your people without having your forsaken study reproaching you, and calling you home, you may easily come to believe that it would be good indeed if you could be one other of two things, and not both; either a preacher or a pastor, but not the two together. But I assure you, you are wrong. The two things are not two, but one...The preacher needs to be a pastor, that he may preach to real men. The pastor must be a preacher, that he may keep the dignity of his work alive. The preacher, who is not a pastor, grows remote; the pastor, who is not a preacher, grows petty. Never be content to let men truthfully say of you, "He is a preacher, but no pastor"; or, "He is a pastor, but no preacher."

He concludes,

> Be both; for you cannot really be one unless you also are the other.[67]

So, with Moses and Ezra we see an Old Testament contribution to the total Biblical picture: Prophet and Pastor-Teacher. We now turn to the New Testament witness.

THE NEW TESTAMENT WITNESS TO PREACHING

A survey of preaching in the New Testament (a recommended task for any preacher who is serious about his calling) reveals a rich feast, indeed. For this study, however, let me give you a few comments from the categories of Jesus as Preacher, Apostolic Preaching, and the Teaching of the Pastoral Epistles on Preaching. There would be more to say from the general epistles on the matter, but I will pick up on some of that (James 3.1 in particular) when I get to The Preacher's Vocation.

THE LORD JESUS CHRIST AS PREACHER

When we consider our Lord's priorities in his ministry, we find that while He performed miracles, He did so, but as Lloyd-Jones says, the miracles were "secondary".[68] Secondary to what? To preaching.

Jesus came preaching. This is the message of St. Matthew and St. Mark and St. Luke:

> and Jesus went about all Galilee, teaching in their synagogues, and preaching the gospel of the kingdom, and healing all manner of sickness and all manner of disease among the people. (Matthew 4:23,KJV)

---

[67] Philip Brooks, Lectures on Preaching (E.P. Dutton, 1877), 75-77

[68] Preachers and Preaching, 20.

> and in the morning, rising up a great while before day, he went out, and departed into a solitary place, and there prayed. and Simon and they that were with him followed after him. and when they had found him, they said unto him, All [men] seek for thee. and he said unto them, Let us go into the next towns, that I may preach there also: for therefore came I forth. and he preached in their synagogues throughout all Galilee, and cast out devils. (Mark 1.35-39, KJV)

> The Spirit of the Lord [is] upon me, because he hath anointed me to preach the gospel to the poor; he hath sent me to heal the brokenhearted, to preach deliverance to the captives, and recovering of sight to the blind, to set at liberty them that are bruised. (Luke 4.18, KJV)

Jesus resisted anything that hindered His primary ministry of preaching. From the temptations of Satan[69], to the possible curtailing of his preaching ministry from those who had been healed[70], to the unwillingness to become embroiled in hearing and rendering decisions in ethical cases.[71] No, Jesus stuck to His primary mission.

and that mission was preaching. Jesus Christ is the greater Prophet whom the Old Testament anticipates. He is The Preacher Of The Ages. If we knew nothing more of preaching in the New Testament other than Jesus did it, it would so elevate that occupation and forever fill it with dignity and honor that it should still be the highest of all callings.

But we do know more.

---

[69] "Then was Jesus let up of the Spirit into the wilderness to be tempted of the devil." (Matthew 4.1, KJV). (see also Mark 1.12, Luke 4.1).

[70] "And Jesus saith unto him, See thou tell no man; but go Thy way, show thyself to the priest, and offer the gift that Moses commanded, for a testimony unto them." (Matthew 8.4,KLV). (See also Mark 5.43; Luke 5.14).

[71] "And he said unto him, Man, who made me a judge or a divider over you?" (Luke 12.14,KJV).

APOSTOLIC PREACHING

The New Testament Scriptures are filled with the preaching of the Apostles. Particularly in Acts do we see the ministry of preaching coming alive before us. What do we learn?

PREACHING IS PRIORITY IN THE CHURCH

The first great act of the Church filled with the Spirit of God was to preach. Peter stood up and followed the coming of the Spirit with evidence of his own anointing. He preached to those amazed onlookers and deftly used the Scriptures of the Old Testament, history, admonition, declarations, appeals, proofs, and Gospel charges to preach Jesus as "Lord and Christ".[72]

Perhaps, though, no greater testimony to the priority of preaching can be found in the apostolic witness than in Acts 6.1-7. During the midst of great growth in the church (verse 1), a dispute arose concerning a mercy ministry and an administrative matter. The twelve Apostles determined that their priority was "prayer and the ministry of the Word (verse 4)." The congregation appointed seven others, then, to do the work of mercy ministry. This move resulted in a great explosion of growth in the disciples of Christ. Never doubt that the priority of ministry is the Word and Prayer. When your church experiences growth and you are tempted to do this, that and the other to keep it all going, recognize that such a scheme smells like smoke! Satan wants ministers doing everything else in the Church but studying the Word, praying over it, teaching it, and helping the saints to apply it! Don't give in! Preach the Word! Make it priority!

PREACHING CARRIES AUTHORITY IN THE CHURCH

Peter was anointed by Christ to preach. His call for them to "repent and let every one of you be baptized in the name of Jesus Christ for the remission of sins" carries authority. In Acts 3.4-5 Peter demands attention from a lame beggar and orders him to stand up after having offered him the Gospel. Peter declares that there is no other name under heaven whereby men may be saved. There is no appeal to reason, no accommodation to other religions, no acquiescing to the powers in place. "The Rock" was preaching the Word of God.

---

[72] "Therefore let all the house of Israel know assuredly, that God hath made that same Jesus, whom ye have crucified, both Lord and Christ." (Acts 2.36, KJV).

There is a church in Colorado Springs called "Pulpit Rock Church". I think that is an odd name for a church, but an apt metaphor for preaching. The pulpit is a rock.[73] Jesus Christ has given authority to His preachers to herald the Kingdom of God and to teach men whatsoever He has commanded them.

PREACHING CALLS FOR CHANGE IN THE LISTENERS

The great message of the kerygma is to "repent and believe" that Jesus Christ rose again from the dead. This is the message of the Apostles and the message we have today. It is a hortatory message. It is direct and seeks affirmation on the part of the listener. It calls for change.

Dr. Robert Rayburn, the great preaching professor and founder of Covenant College and Seminary, used to tell his preaching students to always imagine him sitting on the back pew of their church with his arms tightly folded over his chest and a smirk on his face – asking "So, what do you want me to do?" I have talked with several older preachers who had Rayburn, and they testify to the effectiveness of that challenge from their old professor. It makes them communicate the requirement for change from the text.

Preaching requires something of the listener.

The business of preaching is not for the timid and the weak. It is a man's business. It is the work of one who has been to the mountain to meet with God and who has a fresh message from Him.

THE PASTORAL EPISTLE'S TEACHING ON THE MATTER OF PREACHING

The New Testament witness, aside from the Gospel accounts of the preaching ministry of our blessed Lord, is rich, indeed, and there is no greater grasp of preaching to be had than in the letters of Paul the Apostle to Timothy and Titus. Timothy was stationed in Ephesus and struggling with a ministry there, and Titus was laying foundations for the church on the island of Crete. There is much to learn here about preaching. Perhaps, the culminating message of the subject is a good way to begin. It is a message preached today at ordinations, seminary graduations and installations.

---

[73] I would keel over if I learned that the pulpit was Plexiglas! One day I will go in and see!

> I charge [thee] therefore before God, and the Lord Jesus Christ, who shall judge the quick and the dead at his appearing and his kingdom; Preach the word; be instant in season, out of season; reprove, exhort with all long-suffering and doctrine. (2 Timothy 4.1-2, KJV).

The Pastoral Epistles are so-called because they contain a message of instruction to fledgling pastors named Timothy and Titus and because they contain a vital message for every preacher since Timothy. No minister of the Gospel should undertake the high and holy work of preaching without a firm grounding in what St. Paul taught about it.

Let every preacher and want-to-be preacher give heed to the Holy Spirit's instruction from the pen of St. Paul and learn well several requirements of preaching:

PREACHING IS CENTERED UPON FAITH IN JESUS CHRIST

> Paul, an apostle of Jesus Christ by the commandment of God our Savior, and Lord Jesus Christ, [which is] our hope; Unto Timothy, [my] own son in the faith: Grace, mercy, [and] peace, from God our Father and Jesus Christ our Lord. As I besought thee to abide still at Ephesus, when I went into Macedonia, that thou mightest charge some that they teach no other doctrine, (1 Timothy 1.1-3, KJV).

Paul is writing to his son in the faith, Timothy. Timothy is a not only a son by way of his conversion to Christ under Paul's preaching, but is a son by virtue of the fact that he was a preaching apprentice under Father Paul.

This letter is designed to instruct Timothy in the entire pastoral ministry and specifically how to deal with situations and problems at the church in Ephesus. You will note that Paul begins his letter with the greeting that centers upon the "Grace, mercy and peace" found in God our Father and Jesus Christ our Savior.

Paul begins an instruction on pastoral theology with an emphasis upon the three sparkling gems of our salvation—grace, mercy and peace—and so must every preacher.

Preaching is centered on redeeming men and women and boys and girls from the destructive cycle of sin and its awful consequences through the proclamation of restoration with God the Father. The restoration is found in God's grace in sending His Son, Jesus Christ to be our Savior from sin. The outcome of that restoration is peace with God.

If a man's preaching ministry does not contain that, it may be properly asked, "Is this Christian preaching?"

> As I besought thee to abide still at Ephesus, when I went into Macedonia, that thou mightest charge some that they teach no other doctrine, Neither give heed to fables and endless genealogies, which minister questions, rather than Godly edifying which is in faith: [so do]. (1 Timothy 1.3-4, KJV)

PREACHING REQUIRES PRESENCE

> As I besought thee to abide still at Ephesus, when I went into Macedonia, that thou mightest charge some that they teach no other doctrine, (1 Timothy 1.3, KJV)

Paul ordered Timothy to remain in Ephesus. No work can be done without a commitment to stay in one place. This is not to invalidate other forms of the preaching ministry such as evangelistic crusades. That sort of work is akin to the apostolic work of St. Paul, himself. What is under consideration at this point, though, is the necessity of pastoral preaching. Someone—and I would say that it is the norm and the majority work—someone must tend the flock. Someone must be in the pulpit week-in and week-out.

Dr. James M. Boice came to the venerable pulpit of Tenth Presbyterian Church in Philadelphia, Pennsylvania in 1968. The church, located as it is in a downtown urban area, might not seem the best spot for a young preacher with a family to rear. But Boice, along with several other pastors in the area, covenanted to stay, no matter what, and till the field of souls of that area. The outcome has been nothing short of remarkable and the ministry of Boice and Tenth Presbyterian is a model for all of us.

Go to your Ephesus and your Philadelphia and till the fields in that community until God, Himself, providentially orders you to another post. This is a requirement in preaching when we speak of preachers as pastors, which, again, is the majority of preachers.

PREACHING REQUIRES THEOLOGICAL UNDERSTANDING

> Desiring to be teachers of the law; understanding neither what they say, nor whereof they affirm. (1Timothy 1.7, KJV)

Boice has written that preaching is the

> ...exposition of a text of Scripture in terms of contemporary culture with the specific goal of helping people to understand and obey the truth of God. But to do that well the preacher must be well studied.[74]

We are increasingly hearing of preachers who dress up in uniforms, employ the techniques of the theatre and Hollywood to get attention.

We have far too many actors in the pulpit today. We have too many preachers who have desired to be teachers, like the fallacious Ephesians, without understanding of what they preach.

Preaching requires scholarship. Preaching requires study. Preaching requires knowledge of theology and history and a life-long pursuit of the truths of the Word of God. Preaching is not to be entered into lightly, and the dignity of the Christian pulpit must never be surrendered to clowns who understand neither what they say or the things which they affirm.

---

[74] James Montgomery Boice, "The Preacher and Scholarship" in *The Preacher and Preaching* (Presbyterian and Reformed, 1986), 91.

PREACHING REQUIRES THAT THE PREACHER BE A MAN WHO KNOWS GOD'S GRACE.

> and I thank Christ Jesus our Lord, who hath enabled me, for that he counted me faithful, putting me into the ministry; Who was before a blasphemer, and a persecutor, and injurious: but I obtained mercy, because I did [it] ignorantly in unbelief. and the grace of our Lord was exceeding abundant with faith and love which is in Christ Jesus. (1 Timothy 1.12-14, KJV)

Many have heard, "they don't care what you know, they just want to know that you care." It is true. I once heard an older preacher remind seminarians that preachers must

> ...preach to the broken hearts in the pew and you will never lack for an interested congregation.

The biographer of that indefatigable old Methodist bishop William A. Quayle wrote,

> William Alfred Quayle was a preacher. He was a preacher from compulsion. His preaching broke out of his soul.[75]

We must have preachers like that today. Is your preaching an extension of your soul on fire for God? Can you say with Jeremiah that you have a "burning fire shut up in your bones" which compels you to preach?[76] Is this not the passion exhibited in Paul's words when he declared,

> For though I preach the gospel, I have nothing to glory of: for necessity is laid upon me; yea, woe is unto me, if I preach not the gospel! (1 Corinthians 9.16, KJV)

To reach people with the message of grace necessarily demands that the preacher have experienced grace. It is one thing to speak about

---

[75] William A. Quayle, Warren Wiersbe, Editor, The Pastor-Preacher (Baker, 1979 reprint with a new introduction), 10.

[76] "Then I said, I will not make mention of him, nor speak any more in his name. But [his word] was in mine heart as a burning fire shut up in my bones, and I was weary with forbearing, and I could not [stay]." (Jeremiah 20.9, KJV)

grace from an intellectual point of view. It reaches the mind of the hearer. It is another thing to demonstrate the wonder of grace by showing in word and spirit that you have encountered God's grace personally.

Michael Horton wrote a book called, Putting the Amazing Back into Grace. We need to put Amazing Grace back into preaching.

TO PREACH IS TO ENGAGE IN WARFARE

> This charge I commit to you, my son Timothy, according to the prophecies previously made concerning you, that by them you may wage the good warfare. (1 Timothy 1.18, NKJV)

You will forgive me if I borrow a word from the vernacular, but this passage is teaching that preaching is not the work for a wimp.

Bishop Quayle wrote:

> It takes more courage to be a preacher than to be a gladiator, or a stormer of fortresses, because the preacher's battle is ever on, never ceases, and lacks the tonic of visible conquest.[77]

PREACHING MUST INVOLVE INSTRUCTION

> If thou instruct the brethren in remembrance of these things, thou shalt be a good minister of Jesus Christ, nourished up in the words of faith and of good doctrine, whereunto thou hast attained. (1 Timothy 4.6, KJV)

While preaching is not teaching, per se, it involves, yea, it finds its very meaning in the doctrine of the Apostles.

Our words "teaching" and "doctrine" are in the New Testament identical. The Apostle's doctrine of Acts 2.42 is our message and the work of our ministry.

> and they continued steadfastly in the apostle's doctrine...

---

[77] William A. Quayle, Warren Wiersbe, Editor, The Pastor-Preacher.

We teach Christ and Him crucified. Preaching is consumed with doctrine. There are many different types of sermon structure, including one that is specifically called doctrinal preaching, but make no mistake about it: all preaching that is Christian preaching is doctrinal.

PREACHING REQUIRES PRACTICE

> Till I come, give attendance to reading, to exhortation, to doctrine. Neglect not the gift that is in thee, which was given by prophecy, with the laying on of the hands of the presbytery. (1 Timothy 4.13-14, KJV).

Paul admonished Timothy to practice the essentials of his ministry. Reading, exhortation and doctrine. Preaching requires practice. It is possible to learn a language and then, out of neglect, to lose that language. The same is true with preaching.

I once heard of an old Pentecostal preacher from South Louisiana. He had a heart attack and was rushed to the hospital for emergency surgery. He had not missed a Sunday's preaching in countless years. But that Sunday he was providentially hindered. When he woke up in the recovery room, his first reaction was deep down concern about whether one Sunday out of the pulpit, one instance of neglecting the preaching ministry, would cost him his calling. So, he called for a nurse. He asked the nurse for a Bible. She thought he was crazy but happily conceded to him. He guided her with clear instruction through the pages of the sacred volume. "Turn to the back of the Bible, now move on through, move further, keep going. There!"

The weak, but spirited old preacher tried to sit up just a fraction and he lifted a trembling, old finger to the passage he knew so well.

> Read that...please...its very important to me.

The old preacher's finger had rested on 1 Samuel 17.40. The young nurse began to read:

> Then he took his staff in his hand; and he chose for himself five smooth stones from the brook, and put them in a shepherd's bag, in a pouch which he had, and his sling was in his hand. and he drew near to the Philistine.

The old man's face began to shine as she read. He started to speak...

> "Five smooth stones —Five smooth stones..."

With every repetitive phrase, his voice grew louder.

> Five smooth stones to defeat a big old enemy! I can see David reaching his hand down in that water. I can hear others laughing and mocking him for choosing such a simple arsenal...

He went on until he finished, and he then he sunk down again into his bed. He grinned ear to ear and told the amazed nurse,

> Ma'am, I thought maybe y'all had took my 'unction' out while I was in that operating room. But, praise God, It's still there!

His "unction" came from exercising the gift that was given to Him by God. Preaching takes practice. If you are serious about your calling, then never neglect the gift that is within you.

PREACHING IS ALL PERVASIVE

> Meditate upon these things; give thyself wholly to them; that thy profiting may appear to all. Take heed unto thyself and unto the doctrine; continue in them: for in doing this thou shalt both save thyself, and them that hear thee. (1 Timothy 4.15-16, KJV).

Eugene Peterson, in his Working the Angles: The Shape of Pastoral Integrity,[78] tells us that preachers only do a few things. Preachers spend time in Prayer, in Scripture and in Spiritual Direction. That's about it. But, those three angles make up the whole of our ministry. Each angle takes up our entire lives.

The preacher finds his life fulfilled in the preparing for, brooding over and executing of God's message to modern man. The work consumes him. For those whom God has placed in the preacher's household, his wife and children, they, too, are witnesses to the all-pervasive nature of the preaching ministry. Perhaps it is for that reason that, when uninformed or just plain cantankerous

---

[78] Eugene Peterson, Working the Angles: The Shape of Pastoral Integrity (Eerdmans, 1990).

parishioners say things such as "Well, our pastor doesn't do much..." in the face of a diligent preacher of the Word, his family gets so hurt. They know what few others realize: preaching is the preacher's whole life.

PREACHING REQUIRES TENACITY

> Preach the word; be instant in season, out of season; reprove, rebuke, exhort with all longsuffering and doctrine. For the time will come when they will not endure sound doctrine; but after their own lusts shall they heap to themselves teachers, having itching ears; and they shall turn away [their] ears from the truth, and shall be turned unto fables. But watch thou in all things, endure afflictions, do the work of an evangelist, make full proof of thy ministry. (2 Timothy 4.2-5, KJV).

> These things speak, and exhort, and rebuke with all authority. Let no man despise thee. (Titus 2.15, KJV).

This last truth I bring you is one of the most critical. One can excel at preaching and yet fail as a preacher for lack of tenacity.

Dr. James Kennedy told me once that a minister must "develop an alligator skin." He must, as can be humanly possible, become impervious to the constant attacks of Satan.

He must also, however, guard himself against the seductive forces in this world. Many will seek to move his preaching ministry away from the Word of God and onto something else. Or, they may crave an unhealthy imbalance within the Scriptures: always wanting more on Revelation, more on some ethical issue, more and more on the matter of the charisma. The preacher is charged by the Holy Spirit to withstand such overtures. Guard the integrity of the pulpit.

CONCLUSIONS

Can we justify preaching? Lloyd-Jones asked that question, and today it is a more pressing question that the day in which he posed it.

Modern technology says no. Psychologists and sociologists might say no. Church growth experts might say no.

But the Bible says yes. God justifies preaching. It will never cease to be the prime way that men and women come into and grow in the faith.

I started with Lloyd-Jones in this final section, so let me conclude with him. The "Doctor" warned us of the essential faddish nature of innovative communication devices, of external gadgetry, of avant-garde philosophies and societal whims, and of the permanence of preaching when he wrote:

> The age in which we are living is so similar to the first century in many respects. The Old World was exhausted then. The flowering period of Greek philosophy had come and gone, Rome in a sense had passed her zenith, and there was the same kind of tiredness and weariness; with consequent turning to pleasure and amusement. The same is true today; and so far from saying that we must have less preaching and turn more and more to other devices and expedients, I say that we have a heaven-sent opportunity for preaching.[79]

As you leave a career to follow a call, remember that you are God's ambassador with heaven's message of a Savior for times like these.

Amen.

---

[79] Preachers and Preaching, 42.

GOD IS CALLING FAITHFUL MEN
©1993 Michael A. Milton

A hymn written by the author for those called to preach and suitable for occasional services of ordination, graduation, and installation

NOTE: The hymn may be sung to the tune DIX 7.7.7.7.7.7 (the traditional tune to "For the Beauty of the Earth") by Conrad Kocher (1838).

God is calling faithful men,
Shepherds for His flock to tend;
His the vision, He ordains,
He supplies and He sustains;
God is calling faithful men,
Shepherds for His flock to tend.

Grounded in His Word, their light,
Out they go into the night;
Seeking lambs who've gone astray,
Leading them back to the Way;
God is calling faithful men,
Shepherds for His flock to tend.

Let not many teachers be,
Greater judgments will they see,
But, as they do heed God's call,
Christ becomes their all in all;
God is calling faithful men,
Shepherds for His flock to tend.

Men led by a nail-pierced hand,
Let them pastor in our land,
Feeding us with tender care,
Word and Sacrament and Prayer;
God is calling faithful men,
Shepherds for His flock to tend.

SOME FURTHER READING PRIOR TO SEMINARY

A Brief List with Annotations

To dig deeper into the matter of vocation and seminary and ordained ministry, I would advise you to follow what Christian author George Grant calls "the footnote trail." As you read, make occasional stops at the bottom of the page and begin to detect, most often, deeper, richer veins of wisdom. Some of the books I've mentioned in my footnotes are out of print, but the used bookstores and sites on the web will be of help.

I offer this list, then, in addition to those footnotes, to help augment your reading. I have included only a few selections here, but within their relatively few pages I believe that most sojourners can find reliable signposts for their journey.

Of course, I would advocate reading with a heart filled with prayer and with frequent petitions to Jesus Christ our Lord, who calls His own into His harvest fields.

Gary D. Badcock, The Way Of Life: A Theology Of Christian Vocation (Wm. B. Eerdmans, 1998). This is a thorough treatment of the matter and contains a helpful bibliography.

Richard Baxter, The Reformed Pastor (Banner of Truth, 1981). You will probably read this in seminary anyway, but why not start now with, in the opinion of many, the premier work on the life and work of a pastor. Baxter is the embodiment of what it means to be an undershepherd of Christ.

Edmund Clowney, Called To The Ministry (Presbyterian and Reformed, 1964). This little book is one of the finest volumes on the subject that I have ever read. It is essential for every one considering the call to ministry. I am certain that I am not the only minister who points to Clowney and to this book as a divining rod that led me to the refreshing waters of service to Jesus Christ.

Os Guinness, The Call: Finding and Fulfilling The Central Purpose Of Your Life (Word Books, 1998). This is a recent and worthy offering on the more general matter of vocation. It helps to smash latent clericalism in our thinking and advances a strong Biblical worldview on the meaning of vocation.

John Hendrix, Finding Your Place In Ministry (Convention Press, 1994). This is a publication by the Southern Baptists that really helps. I know. Mine is all marked up from my own explorations. It is essentially a workbook that helps guide you through the vocational wardrobe of the ministry and allows you to try on a few hats for size. After taking the inventories, I have felt, in retrospect, that Hendrix's advice was good advice. This is a good companion to my article in this book, "What Color is Your Pulpit?"

Eugene Peterson, Working The Angles (Wm. B. Eerdmans, 1987). Peterson is one of my all time favorites. He speaks my language, but in words that stir me and convict me, and, in the end, teaches me. I could easily urge you to go and get all that Peterson has ever written and begin to drink deeply and learn what a pastor is all about. But, you have much to read and, further, you must be about leaving your career to follow your call. Therefore, I recommend starting with this one. The angles of the pastorate, according to Peterson, are prayer, Scripture, and spiritual direction. After you are in the pastorate for a few years, take a holiday with Under The Unpredictable Plant (Wm. B. Eerdmans, 1992) and get ready to repent and to renew. All of Peterson's works are fine traveling companions for the road before you. He is a great practitioner of the pastorate and has, since his retirement, truly become the pastor's friend.

Charles H. Spurgeon, Lectures To My Students (Zondervan, 1980 reprint). This is the complete and unabridged version of C.H. Spurgeon's actual lectures to his ministerial students at Spurgeon College. Why read this now? First and foremost, you should read it to experience the thrill of sensing the raw-bone Saxon English of this British pulpit lion. Secondly, this book will whet your appetite for the actual classroom. I thank my pastor who gave it to me prior to seminary. I arrived with great expectations for study and with a big vision for the work before me. Of course, if you have never read Spurgeon, this will excite your soul for more. There's plenty out there and the old master will seldom disappoint you.

Benjamin B. Warfield, The Religious Life Of The Theological Student (Presbyterian and Reformed, 1992 reprint). This is the classic treatment of the subject, and a fine pastoral treatment of the student's soul from a famous if not quintessential seminary professor of yesteryear.

INDEX

A

Abraham, 13, 21, 22, 46, 60
academic, 39, 44, 54, 80
academic excellence, 44
administrator, vii, 78, 79
Andrew, 24, 26
Apostle, 33, 38, 60, 73, 91, 93, 95, 97, 100, 120, 125
Apostles, 13, 19, 60, 119, 120, 125
appointments, 46, 54
Army chaplains, 79, 81, 91, 92

B

Badcock, Gary D., 131
Baptist, viii
Barnabas, 38, 77
Baxter, Richard, 116, 131
Baxter, Robert E., 9
Bethel, 13
Bible, 13, 21, 32, 39, 66, 67, 75, 96, 103, 104, 105, 108, 110, 111, 112, 126, 129; Biblical, vii
Biblical, vii, 20, 31, 56, 111, 117, 132. See Bible
Boice, James M., 122, 123
boss, 17, 28
Bush, George - President of the United States, 21
business, 21, 24, 25, 31, 37, 41, 54, 56, 58, 65, 75, 86, 96, 99, 102, 104, 120

C

Calhoun, David, ix
calling, vii, 12, 13, 19, 20, 22, 23, 24, 25, 26, 27, 35, 38, 43, 63, 68, 72, 73, 74, 77, 80, 87, 88, 92, 102, 109, 110, 116, 117, 126, 127. See also vocation
calls, 23, 24, 25, 28, 34, 41, 58, 70, 71, 75, 91, 103, 110, 111, 113, 120, 131
Calvin, John, 13, 14
Calvinist, 43
campus, 45, 47, 71
candidacy, viii
candidates, vii, 23, 43, 58
candidates for the ministry, 58
Capon, Robert Farrarr, 16
career, vii, viii, x, xi, 12, 19, 20, 21, 23, 26, 28, 30, 31, 32, 34, 39, 40, 41, 42, 45, 48, 49, 50, 52, 53, 56, 58, 70, 92, 93, 97, 98, 132; careers, viii, 25
carpenter, 27, 100
carpentry, 27
Chambers, Oswald, x
chaplain, 71, 78, 79, 81, 91
children, vii, 17, 20, 23, 48, 51, 52, 68, 105, 112, 127
Choosing a seminary, 42
Christ, 16, 17, 23, 24, 25, 26, 30, 32, 33, 34, 36, 37, 38, 39, 42, 46, 47, 54, 58, 59, 60, 62, 63, 68, 72, 77, 78, 88, 90, 91, 92, 94, 97, 100, 101, 106, 109, 110, 113, 119, 121, 124, 126, 131
Christian, x, 12, 13, 21, 35, 53, 62, 63, 64, 75, 79, 93, 106, 122, 123, 126, 131
Christian radio. See
Christian service, 12, 21, 63
Chrysostom, 67
Church, vii, viii, 16, 17, 18, 31, 33, 38, 39, 43, 47, 49, 59, 66, 67, 71, 77, 92, 93, 101, 102, 103, 104,

INDEX

105, 106, 107, 108, 109, 111,
119, 120, 122, 128
church planter, vii, 62, 71, 76, 77,
78, 96
church planters, 76, 78
churches, 45, 46, 73, 74, 76, 79, 95,
102, 105, 106, 108
clericalism, vii, 107, 132
Clowney, Edmund, vii, 12, 18, 62,
111, 113, 131
commandments, 28, 112
computer, 39, 79
confessions, theological, 44
congregation, 17, 29, 44, 49, 74, 75,
114, 119, 124
Coral Ridge Presbyterian Church,
Fort Lauderdale, FL, x
costs of seminaries, 52
councils of local churches, 45
counsel, 32, 35, 59
counseling, vii, 27, 38, 56, 92
Couples, vii
Covenant College, Lookout
Mountain, TN, 101, 120
Covenant Theological Seminary, St.
Louis, MO, 101
craftsman, 27, 39
credentials, 71
customers, 27, 51

D

Damascus, 14, 38, 77
daughter, 17, 28, 30, 49, 50, 51
David, 60, 102, 103, 104, 127
dead bury the dead, 37, 41, 52
debt, 29, 30, 52
denomination, viii, 17, 19, 39, 43,
71, 95
departmental ministry, 76
difficult people in the church, 93
DISC personality profile instrument,
73
discontentment. See . See. See
Distance learning, 45, 46
Doctor of Philosophy, Ph.D., 80
Doctor of Theology, Th.D., 80
Doctrinal Integrity, 43

E

ecclesiastical, 30, 46

economics, 28
education, 22, 25, 43, 44, 46, 75, 87,
91, 103
egalitarianism, vii, 107, 108
Eli, 34
employers, 24, 45
environment, 33, 57, 75
Ephesus, 91, 120, 121, 122
Episcopal, viii
Episcopal Church, 16
Episcopal rector, 52
Episcopal Theological School, 20
equip, 24, 47, 75
eternal life, 58, 59, 64, 68, 98
eternity, 41
Evangelism Explosion, 16, 17
evangelist, 71, 78, 79, 128
exile, 22, 23, 24
Exodus, 22, 23, 111
experience, viii, x, 17, 21, 25, 29, 33,
45, 47, 53, 73, 132

F

faculty, 43, 64, 99
failure, 78, 97
faithfulness, 26, 47, 49
families, 28, 45, 77, 81, 97, 102
family, viii, 17, 20, 21, 22, 23, 26,
28, 29, 30, 33, 35, 37, 42, 45, 46,
48, 49, 50, 51, 52, 53, 59, 78, 83,
122, 128
family life, 48
father, 21, 30, 36, 103, 122
fathers of the early Church, 67
fellowship, 53
first careers, 25, 48
fishermen, 24, 25, 26
foreign missionaries, 78
formation, seminary as, 49
Fortune 500, vii, x, 17, 19
founders, 61
friends, 53
fulfillment, 63, 70, 113
full time service, 25
full-time, working, 29

G

Gadarene demoniac, 33
Galilee, Sea of, 24
General Call, 12

Genesis, 21
gifts, spiritual, 13, 33, 38, 39, 56, 63, 70, 71, 72, 73, 74, 78, 86
God, vii, x, xi, 12, 13, 15, 16, 17, 18, 19, 21, 22, 23, 24, 25, 26, 27, 28, 29, 30, 32, 33, 34, 35, 36, 37, 38, 39, 41, 42, 43, 44, 47, 48, 49, 51, 52, 53, 54, 57, 58, 59, 60, 63, 64, 65, 66, 67, 68, 69, 70, 71, 72, 73, 76, 77, 79, 86, 87, 88, 90, 91, 92, 93, 94, 95, 96, 97, 98, 99, 100, 104, 105, 106, 108, 109, 110, 111, 112, 113, 114, 115, 119, 120, 121, 122, 123, 124, 125, 127, 129
God's people, 24
God's time, 24
Gospel, x, 16, 18, 19, 22, 23, 24, 25, 28, 37, 39, 46, 47, 48, 51, 53, 56, 58, 63, 64, 69, 70, 71, 72, 79, 80, 92, 93, 97, 104, 106, 119, 120, 121
grace, 16, 19, 23, 27, 33, 42, 54, 58, 62, 72, 73, 77, 92, 95, 121, 122, 124, 125
graduate school, 44, 51
Great Commission, 16, 94
Greek philosophy, 129
Guinness, Os, 104, 132

H

happiness, 59
harvest fields, 76, 131
headmaster of a Christian school, 62
Health, 29
Hebrew, 53, 98
heed the call, 32, 63
Hendrix, John, 132
homemaker, 25
Hound of Heaven, 15, 17

I

identity, 23, 56, 57, 59
inner city, 77
institution, 31, 51, 64, 79
institutional chaplain, 78
international, 31
Internet, 46, 47
internship, 29, 52, 83
Inward call, 15

Isaiah, 27, 60, 113
itinerant evangelists, 76

J

Jacob, xi
James, 24, 26, 54, 101, 115, 117, 122, 123, 128
Jeremiah, 46, 60, 124
Job Opportunities, 45
John, 13, 14, 24, 26, 36, 44, 54, 101, 104

K

Kellogg Lectures, 20
Kennedy: D. James Kennedy, x
kingdom of God, 22, 24, 25, 36, 37, 60, 76, 77, 78, 117, 121
Knox Seminary, xi, 29
Kubler-Ross, Elizabeth, 85

L

labor, 27, 47, 53, 92, 96
laborers, 26, 32, 36, 63
law, 58, 114, 115, 123
Law School, 18
lawyers, 56
layman, vii
leaders, 24, 46, 59, 61, 75, 76, 79, 91, 94, 108
leadership, 21, 22, 29, 38, 71, 74, 75, 80
leaving, viii, x, xi, 20, 26, 28, 34, 41, 46, 48, 53, 56, 70, 132
lectures, 57, 69, 102, 132
lessons, 22, 25, 30
libraries, 46
living water, 59
Lloyd-Jones, David Martyn, 102, 103, 107, 109, 110, 117, 128, 129
local church, 17, 45, 53, 62, 70
Lord, x, 13, 14, 16, 19, 21, 22, 25, 26, 27, 28, 31, 32, 33, 34, 35, 36, 37, 38, 46, 47, 49, 50, 54, 57, 58, 65, 72, 76, 77, 85, 87, 89, 92, 95, 100, 108, 109, 112, 113, 114, 115, 117, 118, 119, 120, 121, 124, 131

Lord of the Harvest, 36, 37, 57, 58
Luke, 24, 35, 36, 37, 39, 52, 54, 113, 117, 118
Luther, Martin, 62, 63

M

Macbeth, 41
manager, vii, x, 17, 25, 29, 39
Mark, 24, 33, 88, 117, 118
marriage, 31, 53, 59, 104
Marris, Peter, 84
Master of Divinity, M.Div., 80
Master of Theology, Th.M., 80
McNeil, John, 13
meaning in life, 59
medicine, 58
Menninger, Dr. Walter, 81, 82, 83, 84, 86, 87
Methodist, 16, 90, 124
mid career transition, 32, 34
Midian, 22
military chaplain, 71
minister, viii, 13, 15, 16, 17, 18, 19, 23, 34, 35, 46, 48, 49, 52, 54, 56, 62, 63, 64, 65, 67, 69, 72, 74, 75, 76, 78, 79, 80, 83, 85, 89, 93, 102, 113, 121, 122, 125, 128, 131
minister of youth, 75
ministerial candidate, 23
ministerial specialties, 56
ministers, 24, 31, 46, 47, 49, 60, 62, 67, 70, 71, 72, 75, 76, 77, 78, 79, 80, 82, 91, 116, 119
Ministry, vii, viii, x, xi, 12, 15, 17, 18, 19, 20, 21, 22, 24, 25, 26, 27, 28, 29, 32, 33, 35, 36, 38, 39, 41, 42, 43, 44, 47, 48, 49, 51, 52, 53, 54, 56, 57, 58, 59, 60, 62, 63, 64, 65, 66, 68, 69, 70, 71, 72, 73, 74, 75, 76, 77, 78, 79, 81, 83, 85, 86, 87, 88, 89, 90, 91, 94, 95, 96, 98, 99, 100, 102, 103, 109, 111, 113, 116, 117, 118, 119, 120, 121, 122, 124, 125, 126, 127, 128, 131, 132
misconceptions about the ministry, 58, 59
missionary, 62, 65, 73, 78
model, viii, 27, 31, 32, 65, 77, 103, 113, 122

money, 29, 59, 102, 104, 107
Moses, 22, 23, 24, 46, 60, 111, 114, 117, 118
Murray, Arthur, x
Myers-Briggs, 73

N

Nazarene, The Church of the, 43
New Testament, 24, 36, 37, 73, 108, 117, 118, 120, 125

O

occupation, 25, 110, 118
way. How is that?, 95
Old Testament, 13, 24, 60, 113, 117, 118, 119
older man, 21
Older Seminarian, 30
opportunities, vii, x, 32, 45, 46, 59, 79
ordained, vii, viii, 17, 18, 23, 24, 32, 33, 34, 35, 39, 47, 56, 70, 71, 74, 79, 80, 107, 108, 115, 131
ordained ministry, vii, viii, 18, 23, 24, 32, 33, 34, 35, 39, 56, 70, 107, 131
organization, 31, 35, 80
outreach, 27
Outward Call, 14, 15

P

para church, 79
parish life, 51
parish work, 47
passion, 16, 17, 22, 23, 33, 44, 72, 73, 74, 75, 78, 79, 80, 91, 99, 100, 124
passionate, 33
pastor, vii, 17, 18, 19, 20, 25, 38, 39, 62, 65, 73, 74, 75, 76, 78, 80, 86, 94, 96, 101, 116, 128, 131, 132;
pastoral, pastors, pastoring, pastored, vii, viii, xi, 48, 52, 54, 74, 75, 109, 116, 121, 122, 133
pastored, 44
pastors, 47, 73, 76, 105, 112, 116, 121, 122, 123

Paul, 14, 15, 18, 26, 33, 34, 38, 46, 60, 63, 65, 66, 68, 72, 73, 77, 91, 94, 97, 98, 99, 100, 109, 110, 120, 121, 122, 124, 126
PCA. See Presbyterian Church in America
Peace Corp, 81, 82
Pentecostal, 126
personal gift inventories, 73
personality inventories, 73
Peter. See . See . See . See . See . See . See
Peterson, Eugene, 127, 132
Ph.D, 30, 85
Philistine, 126
plumber, 25
politician. See
Post Seminary Stress Syndrome, 56, 81, 89
praxis, 44, 45
Praxis and Academic Excellence, 44
prayer, 119, 127
preach, x, 13, 14, 15, 18, 22, 27, 28, 36, 37, 39, 44, 59, 60, 63, 72, 79, 92, 94, 98, 101, 102, 104, 108, 110, 111, 113, 116, 118, 119, 123, 124
preacher, 16, 27, 35, 37, 60, 77, 79, 80, 102, 103, 104, 106, 108, 109, 111, 113, 116, 117, 121, 122, 123, 124, 125, 126, 127, 128
preachers, 37, 44, 57, 71, 90, 102, 103, 106, 110, 111, 112, 113, 116, 120, 123, 124, 127
preaching, 16, 17, 28, 35, 39, 44, 57, 60, 65, 71, 79, 101, 102, 103, 104, 105, 106, 107, 108, 109, 110, 111, 112, 113, 115, 116, 117, 118, 119, 120, 121, 122, 123, 124, 125, 126, 127, 128, 129
preparation for the call, 41
Presbyterian, x, 12, 17, 71, 101, 111, 122, 123, 131, 132
Presbyterian Church in America, 17, 71, 101
prestige, 58
profession, 25, 26, 91, 99; professions, 25, 26, 68, 91
professionalism, 57, 90, 91
professor, 44, 47, 62, 65, 71, 80, 120, 133

Prophets, 13, 19, 60, 112
Proverbs, 48, 50
psychological tests, 73
psychologist, 30
psychologists, 128
pulpit, 14, 56, 70, 71, 73, 94, 95, 103, 104, 105, 109, 114, 116, 120, 122, 123, 126, 128, 132
pursuit of the call, 41

R

Rayburn, Robert, 101, 120
real estate, 31, 50
Reformed, 12, 17, 43, 111, 116, 123, 131, 132
Reformed Theological Seminary, 43
Reformers, 61
requirements, 30, 43, 121
Reymond, Robert L., 69, 110
Robertson, A.T., 36, 37
Rodenmayer, Robert N.. See . See
Roman Catholic, 85
Romans, 33, 72

S

sacrifice, 19, 31, 62, 85, 100
saints, 24, 74, 75, 91, 96, 119
salary, 77, 102
sales, 25, 35, 45
sales manager, 25
salesman, 25, 29, 31, 39
Samuel, 12, 34, 126
Satan, 88, 92, 118, 119, 128
savings, 52
scholars, 24
school, viii, 18, 29, 30, 39, 43, 44, 50, 51, 52, 53, 62, 68, 78, 80, 83, 99
scouting trip to see prospective seminaries, 50
Scripture, 18, 35, 44, 54, 88, 102, 106, 108, 115, 119, 123, 127, 128, 132
second career, 27
seminarian, vii, viii, 20, 24, 29, 30, 31, 54, 65, 66, 68, 69, 83
seminarians, 20, 30, 34, 42, 50, 53, 58, 64, 67, 81, 82, 83, 101, 124
seminaries, 43, 45, 46, 47, 102, 104

INDEX

seminary, vii, viii, xi, 20, 22, 23, 26, 27, 28, 29, 30, 31, 35, 41, 42, 43, 44, 45, 46, 47, 48, 49, 50, 51, 52, 53, 54, 56, 62, 64, 65, 66, 67, 68, 69, 70, 71, 73, 76, 80, 81, 82, 83, 85, 86, 87, 89, 98, 101, 102, 103, 116, 120, 131, 132, 133
seminary professor, 47
senior minister, vii
senior pastor, 71, 74, 75, 76
sermon, 104, 106, 110, 126
sermons, 27, 51, 57, 78, 87, 94, 103, 105
servanthood, 57, 69, 74, 78
sessions, Presbyterian, 27, 45
Shakespeare, 41
sociologists, 128
solo pastor, 74
son, minister's, 52
Southern Baptist Church, 16
Southern Presbyterian Review, 12
sovereign: sovereignty, xi, 24
Specific Call, 13
Spirit, The Holy Spirit, xi, 36, 54, 87, 88, 95, 100, 113, 118, 119, 121, 128
Spiritual, 34, 127
spiritual direction, 127
spiritual formation, 53
Spurgeon, Charles Haddon, 132
Stott, John, 101, 104
study, 19, 32, 41, 54, 65, 82, 83, 85, 88, 101, 102, 103, 108, 116, 117, 123, 132
success, 57, 59, 96, 97, 99, 100
Sunday, 15, 17, 66, 74, 75, 126
Sunday school, 15, 17, 66
Systematic Theology, 69

T

Tarshish, 18
Taylor, L. Roy, ix
teacher, 17, 39, 62, 65, 78, 80, 109, 110
teachers, 48, 56, 80, 112, 123, 128
Teaching, 26, 80, 117
Technical Call, 13
Technical calling, 13
technology, 104, 128
Tenth Presbyterian Church, 122
term papers, 51

testimony, 18, 24, 26, 41, 52,
theological. See . See . See . See . See . See . See . See . See . See
theology, 12, 32, 39, 42, 44, 66, 69, 74, 86, 121, 123, 131
Theology of Vocation, 12
Thompson, Francis, 15, 17
Timothy, 38, 47, 65, 66, 67, 90, 91, 93, 94, 95, 96, 97, 120, 121, 122, 124, 125, 126, 127, 128
trade, 25, 31
tradesmen, 56
training, 25, 31, 39, 47, 51, 56, 64, 73, 81, 85, 86, 91
transition, 19, 24, 26, 31, 40, 48, 50, 51, 81, 82, 83

U

unction in preaching, 127
undergraduate, 30, 39
United Methodist, 16

V

vision, 20, 44, 47, 70, 76, 77, 78, 79, 83, 85, 132
visitation pastor, 75
visitation, pastoral, 78
vocation, vii, 12, 22, 26, 28, 42, 70, 131, 132
vocational transition, 24, 27

W

Wall Street, 27
Warfield, Benjamin Breckenridge, 132
warnings for the ministry, 74, 75, 80
Wesleyan, 43
wife, vii, 16, 17, 18, 19, 20, 23, 28, 29, 31, 35, 37, 44, 48, 49, 50, 51, 68, 90, 127
witness, 15, 24, 26, 117, 119, 120
Word of God, 12, 17, 18, 25, 26, 28, 29, 37, 42, 48, 65, 71, 88, 90, 91, 92, 96, 102, 103, 105, 107, 108, 110, 111, 112, 113, 114, 115, 119, 123, 128

Y

yoke of Christ, 63

younger minister, 31, 91
younger seminarians, 30
youth, 17, 18, 23, 73

BIBLIOGRAPHY

More Helps for Those Struggling with a Call to the Ministry

This Call's For You: Prize Winning Sermons on Christian Vocation. Louisville: Office of Christian Vocation and Enlistment National Ministries Division Presbyterian Church (U.S.A).

Careers in the Christian Ministry: An Ecumenical Guidebook for Counselors, Pastors, and Youth. (1976). [Wilmington, N.C.]: Consortium Books.

The Pastoral Care of Vocation in the Local Churches. (1983). London: Catholic Truth Society.

Abba, J. (1997). Vocation: Journey to Priesthood and Religious Life. Nsukka, Nigeria: Rise and Shine Publications.

Arnold, K. (2000). On The Way: Vocation, Awareness, and Fly-Fishing. New York: Church Pub.

Azevedo, M. D. C., & Diercksmeier, J. W. (1988). Vocation for Mission: The Challenge of Religious Life Today. New York: Paulist Press.

Balthasar, H. U. V., & Mccarthy, M. F. (1983). The Christian State of Life. San Francisco: Ignatius Press.

Beecher, L. F. (1851). On The Choice of A Profession. An Address Delivered Before the Theological Society of Union College on Sabbath Evening, July 20, 1851. Albany: Weed Parsons.

Bentham, E. (1771). Reflexions Upon The Study of Divinity: to Which Are Subjoined Heads of A Course of Lectures. Oxford: Printed At the Clarendon Press.

Brown, K., & Hoover, J. (1987). It's Never Too Late to Say Yes! : Eleven Inspiring Accounts of People Who Made Midlife Ministry Commitments. Ventura, Calif., U.S.A.: Regal Books.

Butler, J. V., & Pittenger, W. N. (1954). What Is The Priesthood? A Book on Vocation. New York,: Morehouse-Gorham.

Calhoun, R. L., & Young Men's Christian Associations of North America. International Committee. (1943). God and The Day's Work; Christian Vocation in An Unchristian World. New York,: Association Press Fleming H. Revell Company.

Catholic Church. National Conference of Catholic Bishops. (1971). Study on Priestly Life and Ministry; Summaries of The Ad Hoc Bishops' Subcommittees on History, Sociology. Washington,: National Conference of Catholic Bishops.

_____. (1986). Vocations and Future Church Leadership: The Collegeville Papers, June 9-16, 1986. Washington, D.C.: U.S. Catholic Conference.

Chambers, O. (1997). Approved Unto God: The Spiritual Life of the Christian Worker. Nashville, Tenn.: Discovery House Publishers. Distributed to the Trade by Thomas Nelson Publishers.

Chappell, C. G. (1967). Men That Count. Grand Rapids,: Baker Book House.

Costa, D. M. (1991). The Ministry of God's People. Nashville, TN: Discipleship Resources.

Dabney, R. L., & Presbyterian Church in the Confederate States of America. Presbyterian Committee of Publication. (1861). "What Is A Call to The Gospel Ministry" by R.L. Dabney. Richmond: Presbyterian Committee of Publication.

De Satgé, J. (1976). Letters to an Ordinand : A Study in Vocation. London: S.P.C.K. : Advisory Council For The Church's Ministry.

Evangelical Lutheran Church in America. Division for Ministry., Bouman, W. R., & Setzer, S. M. (1995). What Shall I Say? : Discerning God's Call to Ministry: A Resource From The Division For Ministry, The Evangelical Lutheran Church in America. Chicago: Evangelical Lutheran Church in America.

Fichter, J. H. (1961). Religion as an Occupation; A Study in the Sociology of Professions. [Notre Dame, Ind]: University of Notre Dame Press.

Gandy, D. J., & Barr, L. S. (1992). Guide to Southern Baptist Vocations. Nashville, Tenn.: Convention Press.

Grzybowski, A. (1992). Préparez Le Chemin du Seigneur! : Vocation du Baptiste, Vocation du Baptisé. Paris: Editions Saint-Paul.

Hall, C. P. (1951). The Christian at His Daily Work; The Christian Meaning of Work for Today—With Questions For Self-Examination and Group Discussion. New York: Dept. of the Church and Economic Life Division of Christian Life and Work National Council of the Churches of Christ in The United States of America.

Hall, C. P., & National Council of the Churches of Christ in The United States of America. Dept. of The Church and Economic Life. (1952). Religion in the Day's Work: Handbook for Conferences, Study Courses and Occupational Groups in Churches and Communities. New York: Department of the Church and Economic Life Division of Christian Life and Work National Council of the Churches of Christ in The U.S.A.

Harper-Bill, C. (1991). Religious Belief and Ecclesiastical Careers in Late Medieval England: Proceedings of The Conference Held At Strawberry Hill, Easter, 1989. Woodbridge, Suffolk [England] ; Rochester, NY: Boydell Press.

Hedley, J. C., & Gregory. (1906). Lex Levitarum, Or, Preparation For The Cure of Souls. New York: Benziger.

Heuss, J. (1955). Our Christian Vocation. Greenwich, Conn.,: Seabury Press.

Hoge, D. R., Potvin, R. H., Ferry, K. M., United States Catholic Conference. Office of Research., & Catholic University of America. Center For The Study of Youth Development. (1984). Research on Men's Vocations to The Priesthood and The Religious Life. Washington, D.C. (1312 Massachusetts Ave., N.W., Washington 20005): U.S. Catholic Conference.

Hood, E. P. (1867). Lamps, Pitchers, and Trumpets; Lectures Delivered to Students for the Ministry on the Vocation of the Preacher. London, Jackson,: Walford and Hodder.

Hooker, T. (1638). The Sovles Vocation, Or, Effectval Calling to Christ. London: Printed By John Haviland For Andrew Crooke and Are to Be Sold At The Black Beare in S. Pauls Church-Yard.

Horton, D., Lampe, W. B., Tittle, E. F., & Joint Religious Radio Committee. (1945). Christian Vocation, A Series of Radio Sermons. Boston, Chicago,: The Pilgrim Press.

Kohler, R. F., García, J., & Hepner, T. (1997). The Christian As Minister: An Inquiry Into Ordained Ministry, Commissioned Ministries, and Church Certification in The United Methodist Church (4th Ed.). Nashville, Tenn.: General Board of Higher Education and Ministry United Methodist Church.

Kuhrt, G. W. (2000). An Introduction to Christian Ministry: Following Your Vocation in the Church of England. London: Church House.

Latourette, K. S. (1946). The Gospel, The Church and The World (First Edition. Ed.). New York ; London: Harper & Brothers Pub.

Manna, P., & Mcglinchey, J. F. (1911). The Workers Are Few; Reflections Upon Vocation to The Foreign Missions. Boston, Mass., Society for the Propagation of the Faith.

Martini, C. M. (1987). Drawn to The Lord : Six Stories of Vocation: Maximilian Kolbe, Thérèse of The Child Jesus, Charles De Foucauld, Simone Weil, Giorgio La Pira, Robert and Christine. [Dublin]: Veritas Publications.

Mason, A. J. (1916). Our Place in Christendom Lectures. London: Longmans Green.

Methodist Church (U.S.). Commission on Courses of Study. (1942). What It Takes. Nashville, Tennessee: General Conference Commission on Courses of Study.

Montgomery, F. E. (1981). Pursuing God's Call: Choosing A Vocation in Ministry. Nashville, Tenn.: Convention Press.

Nelson, J. O. (1963). Vocation and Protestant Religious Occupations ([1st] Ed.). New York,: Vocational Guidance Manuals.

Parker, P. (1953). Teaching As A Vocation. London,: Burns Oates.

Preece, G. R. (1998). The Viability of the Vocation Tradition in Trinitarian, Credal, and Reformed Perspective: The Threefold Call. Lewiston, NY ; Queenston ; Lampeter: Edwin Mellen Press.

Presbyterian Church (U.S.A.). Office of Communication. (2000). Got A Call? [Louisville, Ky.]: Office of Theological Education Presbyterian Church (U.S.A.).

Proctor, S. D., & Taylor, G. C. (1996). We Have This Ministry: The Heart of The Pastor's Vocation. Valley Forge, PA: Judson Press.

Quayle, W. A. (1918). The Dynamite of God. New York, Cincinnati,: The Methodist Book Concern.

Rose, B. L. (1967). Confirming Your Call in Church, Home, and Vocation. Richmond,: John Knox Press.

Rossman, P., & Noyce, G. B. (1985). Helping People Care on the Job. Valley Forge, PA: Judson Press.

Roth, B. (1998). God's Call and Your Vocation: A Look at Christian Calls and Church Occupations. Nashville, Tenn.: Section of Deacons and Diaconal Ministries Division of Ordained Ministry United Methodist General of Higher Education Ministry.

Scheuerman, E. L. (1998). Recollections of Vocation and Priestly Ministry. Detroit, Mich: E.L. Scheuerman.

Schnase, R. C. (1991). Testing and Reclaiming Your Call to Ministry. Nashville: Abingdon Press.

Smith, B. B. (1850). Special Vocation of The Protestant Episcopal Church in These United States: A Sermon Preached At The Opening of The General Convention, in Christ Church, Cincinnati, Wednesday, October 2, 1850. Philadelphia: King & Baird Printers.

Snow, J. H. (1988). The Impossible Vocation: Ministry in the Mean Time. Cambridge, Mass.: Cowley Publications.

_____ (1992). A Vocation to Risk: Notes on Ministry in A Profane World. Cambridge, Mass.: Cowley Publications.

Speyr, A. V., Balthasar, H. U. V., & Mccarthy, M. F. (1986). The Christian State of Life. San Francisco: Ignatius Press.

Trueblood, E. (1952). Your Other Vocation ([1st] Ed.). New York,: Harper.

Turner, H. J. M. (1990). Ordination and Vocation, Yesterday and Today: Current Questions About Ministries in The Light of Theology and History. Worthing, West Sussex, England: Churchman Publishing.

Tweedy, H. H., & YMCA of The USA. (1922). Christian Work As A Vocation. New York,: The Macmillan Company.

White, A. G. (1974). A Career in the Ministry. Sound Recording. New York,: J. Norton Publishers.

Whitelaw, D. (1996). Maps & Models for Ministry. San Diego, Calif.: Point Loma Press.

Young, P. (1817). A Brief Account of the Life and Experience, Call to the Ministry, Travels and Afflictions of Peter Young, Preacher of the Gospel in Two Parts. Portsmouth, N.H.: Printed By Beck & Foster.

ABOUT THE AUTHOR

The author, Michael A. Milton, earned the Doctor of Philosophy degree in Theology and Religious Studies from the University of Wales, Lampeter. His dissertation advisers were The Reverends Dr. Noel Gibbard and Canon William Price. The research centered on theological and political controversies in 17th century Puritanism. His Master of Divinity degree was received cum laude from Knox Theological Seminary in Fort Lauderdale, Florida, and he holds the BA from Mid America Nazarene University, Olathe, Kansas. Following a career that included training as an Albanian interpreter in the United States Navy, and sixteen years of service for two FORTUNE 500 companies, the author surrendered to the call to preach the Gospel of Jesus Christ. Ordained in the Presbyterian Church in America, his ministerial record includes the founding of two churches and a Christian school, and administering a graduate school of theology. He presently pastors one of the churches he planted, Kirk O' the Isles Presbyterian Church, in Savannah, Georgia, and is the speaker on The Living Word radio ministry. Serving at various levels in his denomination and on the boards of several Christian organizations, the author is also Adjunct Professor at Knox Theological Seminary (FL), Erskine Theological Seminary (SC), and is a US Army Reserve Chaplain. Dr. Milton, active in the Evangelical Theological Society, is a regular writer for The Christian Observer magazine and has published articles in World Magazine, Preaching Magazine, Preaching Online, PCANews.Com, and The Journal of The Evangelical Theological Society.

This is his first book. The author resides with his wife, Mae, and son, John Michael, at their home on Skidaway Island, Georgia.

www.ingramcontent.com/pod-product-compliance
Lightning Source LLC
Chambersburg PA
CBHW072148160426
43197CB00012B/2295